The Scent of Rosemary

A Memoir

Olga Lucía Mutis Peralta

Translation of *Memorias con olor a romero*

By Andrew Klatt

This is an intelligent book. If you place a mobile phone in front of the QR codes within its pages, you can listen to the favorite songs of the book's characters.

https://www.youtube.com/watch?v=ND54Wg7k37M

Vivencias santandereanas (Lyrics by César Ardila Castro, Music by Víctor Hugo Suárez)

Dedication

To Billy, whose inner light illuminates my life.

https://www.youtube.com/watch?v=pVeBr8iengY

Mi Luz (Mr. Frank)

Prologue

When I was little, I used to ask myself Why am I here? Sometimes this was out of despair, other times out of desperation or simple curiosity. I asked myself other questions of the kinds that many do, such as if God made the world, who made God, or why there are social, racial, and religious differences. Why do some people die young and others live long lives? Why, God, did you send me to this family?

I'm sixty-six years old now, yet I haven't found answers to many of these questions. On the other hand, I don't need the answers as much as I once did. I know that we're here to live in a way that will bring us closer to God (Feel free to call the divine being your Higher Power, Spirit, the Universe, or whatever name your religion uses. I continue to call this entity God. This is the name that comes most easily to me, although my conception is less restrictive that of the nuns who taught me). The reward for a life well lived will be to climb a little higher on the spiritual ladder, or to slide back down to square one if we are not up to the task. This is comparable to the game of Chutes and Ladders that we played as children. The difficulty is in deciding whether we want to ascend, and if so, how quickly, because there are many roads to choose from.

I should say that I studied in a Catholic school, and from very early on I rebelled against a religion that spoke to me of punishment, of a God disposed to strike us down with a bolt of lightning if we didn't behave ourselves. I didn't object to the idea of a Heaven where we could go if we said our prayers and cleaned our plates (because that was what any good girl would do), providing we attended mass.

I had no problem with cleaning my plate. In Colombia, that meant eating our soup, because every afternoon we were served soup and *seco*, a plate of meat, chicken, or fish with rice (and lots of sweets, and of course *arepas*), so that was no problem. I learned to pray as though I were

3

conversing with God, without recourse to the rote phrases that have never meant anything to me. The requirement to attend mass was a little more complicated, but I made a deal with God: "Let me off the mass thing and just send me the instruction book that you've owed me since I was born."

And he answered me: "That would be too easy. I'll send you signs, but you'll have to make more of an effort to figure them out for yourself."

~

Motherly Love

(or Lack thereof)

Inés ran playfully all around the house, careful not to make a sound. Her father would get mad if she disturbed him in his home medical office, but she was most concerned not to wake up her mother, who'd finally fallen asleep. Her mother's headaches must have been awful, because the poor thing seemed to be forever despondent and tearful. Fortunately, the medicine that Tutú gave her appeared to help. After she took it, the color returned to her cheeks and she dried her tears. Inés had seen Tutú arrive that day, and she'd seen her mix some powder in water and wait until her father went to his office to bring the mixture to her mother, who waited impatiently. She didn't understand why her father always got so mad when her mother had complaints. He would say

6

something like "I don't like weepy women," and slam the door shut. So, Inés always tried not to cry if she bumped her head or fell down. Papá couldn't stand to see her cry and she didn't want to be weepy like her mother.

When she turned the corner into the hall, she came upon the napping dogs. They didn't want to play with her today, but she didn't mind because she was used to playing alone. What did little girls play if they had sisters and brothers? Probably with some boring dolls, but she had no interest in that. She did have a porcelain doll that was pretty, but it was so pretty that her mother didn't let her touch it because she could break it. If she asked to play with or even pick up the doll, she inevitably got a lecture: "You're a naughty girl; you break whatever we give you."

So she learned to play alone or with the dogs, who never spurned her or called her naughty. And if the dogs didn't want to play—as was the case today—she could always play with imaginary friends, those who stepped out of books to join in her games. Some of them stepped out of medical journals that came to her father from France, so they spoke to her in French. She didn't understand much of their pronunciation, though she could follow what was written in the journals. It wasn't too hard, because the words were like puzzle pieces, and they were used in repetitive patterns. Once you figured out the meaning of a word, you could use it to intuit the meaning of the surrounding words, see where else it was used, and make sense of the phrases on the page. Nobody realized it, but before long she'd learned many words in French. Too bad nobody cared enough to teach her to speak the language. But why should they? Her imaginary friends would eventually disappear, and she wouldn't care anymore what the French people who sometimes joined her games were saying. How did she know they'd eventually disappear? Easy. Her jolly friend who stepped out of the last book she read had told her this would happen. She got quite sad and even tearful, but Tutú told her that good girls shouldn't cry. After she remembered this admonition, she stopped listening to that jolly friend for several days. She couldn't resist his overtures for long, however, because he was so friendly and he always answered her questions.

Sometimes she saw people who said nothing to her, and this was intriguing. For example, when they all went to see the churches decked out for Holy Week, she was left home because she had a slight fever and her father wouldn't let her leave the house. It was true that her body ached, but after a long nap she felt better and began to wander around the house, one of her favorite pastimes. She had been left with Concepción, the cook, but Concepción had fallen asleep in the rocking chair in her room. Inés was accustomed to walking around unnoticed, and she left the room soundlessly without waking her caretaker. The house was silent, but the heat was so oppressive that it was almost audible as it enveloped her like a blanket. She felt the hot air seize her lungs as she inhaled. And she was not the only victim. The dogs lay near the planters of geraniums that bordered the patio, as though drawn to the coolness of the clay. Even the geraniums, known to be heat-resistant, hung lifelessly. The whitewashed walls shimmered and the clay roof tiles made crackling sounds like toasted bread being crushed. Suddenly Inés saw a figure sliding silently along the wall at the end of the corridor. Strangely, though, she didn't hear the sound that clothing normally makes as it brushes along a wall. She ran toward the figure to see it better, but she could only make out that it was a woman wearing espadrilles, with ribbon bows in her long loose braids. When the figure crossed the threshold into a spare room used only to store some infrequently used items, she got a look at her face and noticed that she was wearing a gleaming crucifix. This all happened so fast that she couldn't make out her features. To no avail, she called out for the woman to wait. When Inés got to the door of the room, she hesitated. It was dark inside and she'd never been in there. The door was usually closed, but that day it was open as though inviting her in. A stale smell of abandonment and solitude wafted out of the room, and she didn't like solitude; it frightened her. At that moment, her neck hairs stood on end. Something from inside the room

10

called to her voicelessly, but a mysterious force kept her frozen in place.

Her cries must have woken Concepción, because she emerged from her room, sleepy-eyed and startled, calling the girl's name. "Inés, my *niña*, what are you doing here? It's very hot and you're going to get your fever back. Come into the room where it's cooler. Come and I'll tell you the story about the little pig I had in the country." This enticement was enough to break the spell brought on by the apparition. She obediently turned and took the hand that Concepción held out to her. She wasn't really hearing what was said, though, because her thoughts were still with the braided woman.

As Tutú told her a bedtime story that night, Inés asked who the woman in the room was. Tutú was silent for a few moments. Then she responded emphatically that nobody lived in that room, but she should never go near it again. But Inés was no fool. She immediately knew that Tutú had seen the woman too, and she swore to herself that someday she would get the secret out of her.

The house had so many secrets that sometimes she despaired of learning them all. One day when the examination room was being cleaned, for example, she slipped in without being noticed and stood open-mouthed at everything her father had there, including glass bottles and flasks in the cabinets, strange instruments, overflowing bookcases, and medical devices. Everything was sparkling clean, without a speck of dust. Cleaning this room was the maid's first task every morning and she wasn't done until it was absolutely spotless. The walls were scrubbed every day and whitewashed once a month. A splash of oil was added to the water for mopping the floor to make it shine and to repel insects, and the glass cabinets were cleaned daily with ammonia water. Her father was fanatic about cleanliness. He never tired of repeating that every illness known to man could be attributed to filth, and he didn't flinch at dismissing any cook or housekeeper who didn't bathe twice a day. There was always water and soap to spare in the house, and the doctor always had a vial of alcohol and a box of matches in his pocket. Tutú told her that when he went out to make house calls, he observed the ground carefully as he walked. If he saw a gob of spit, he'd pour a few drops of alcohol on it and light it with a match. Only when he saw that the alcohol was burning would he proceed.

His patients came to him in all conditions on their first visits, but the second time they came they were notably changed. Their faces were scrubbed, their hands were washed, and though their clothes may be torn or raggedy, they were freshly laundered. Inés didn't know what tone he took with them, but she knew he convinced them that cleanliness was of the utmost importance. And they adored, even venerated him. This may have been due to his invariably accurate diagnoses, or because he didn't bother to charge them if he saw that they couldn't pay. But somehow they compensated him, some with a few eggs, others with a hen, a box of pineapples, or a bunch of plantain. Then there were those who brought plants, saying "Sorry I can't give you anymore, Doctor, but this plant is good for rheumatism, and I didn't see one in your garden."

13

Tutú would lovingly plant it in the garden next to the herb that was good for the kidneys, another one that did wonders for the liver, the one that was used to treat stomach pain or diarrhea, and near the rue, the spearmint, and the pennyroyal. They would all grow and thrive under the care of Tutú's unfailingly green thumb.

The kitchen also had well-guarded secrets that Inés discovered little by little, until she learned to cook like her teachers.

But her favorite place was the library, where she shut herself in to pretend that everything in her life was normal. When she picked up a book, it was like falling down a bottomless well from which she would emerge only when summoned to a meal. And in that case it was best that she hurry to the dining room, because the doctor was ill-tempered and impatient.

When her mother was having a good day, she received visitors who told of the trips they'd taken and the parties they'd attended, along with the latest gossip from town, which grew in proportion as they spoke. Sometimes Inés listened from behind a door and imagined that she'd attended those parties wearing pretty dresses sent from Paris that she hardly ever had occasion to wear. Her father could never take her to such parties of course, because he was always so busy, and her mother was always "indisposed."

Sometimes she wanted to rebel, to spread her wings and fly off into the sky, or at least escape the prison that was her house, but any such escapes were strictly limited to her imagination. Her closest allies in these fantasies were characters from books who had the kinds of adventures that were denied to her. They could change their names, change their appearance, and change themselves in unpredictable ways. They could travel to far-off places and come in and out of her life as they wished, but they were ever graven in her photographic memory.

She learned to read French because her limitless appetite for the written word drove her to read whatever came into her hands, be it her mother's fashion magazines or her father's medical journals.

But she was close to eighteen and hadn't learned to love. She had no experience with courtship or even flirtatiousness. She'd never experienced a suggestive brush of the hands, a furtive but meaningful glance, a stolen kiss, or a whispered "I love you."

✿

Her cousin Cecilia had arrived from Bogotá the day before, and as always, she burst into her Uncle Daniel's house like a fresh morning breeze.

She was short and chubby, but her energy was contagious and impossible to resist. Nobody was immune to her charms, including Inés. She adored her cousin and given the opportunity would have followed her to the end of the earth, but today Ceci just wanted to go to the fair. Inés got permission to go, and with everything that people said was there that year, she wouldn't have missed it for the world.

Tutú went with them because it wouldn't be right for them to be seen unaccompanied. She put up a bit of an argument when Cecilia decided to have her fortune read at the gypsy tent, but nothing could stop Ceci. She was a force of nature, so Tutú gave up and waited a few steps away. Ceci paid a few cents for the palm reading, and she was not at all happy with the future predicted for her by the cigar-smoking gypsy woman with bad breath and yellow teeth. Determined to put the experience behind her, she turned on her heel, grabbed at Inés, and pulled her away. Before they had taken two steps, however, another young gypsy called out to them.

"Hey, you with the black eyes!"

They both turned around, but the gypsy looked only at Inés.

"Yes, you. Come back here. I can let you see who you're going to marry, and you don't have to give me anything in addition to what your friend already paid. If you like what I show you, you can buy a carnation from my granny, sitting over there next to that colorful tent."

17

Surprised and curious, they looked over to where the gypsy was pointing and saw a colorful gypsy tent with festive streamers adorning the entrance. Then they saw the old woman with tiered skirts seated on a small stool next to a bucket of red carnations. The woman flashed them a toothless smile and gestured to them to accept the offer.

Somewhat skeptically, they approached the young gypsy, but she didn't let Cecilia come any closer:

"What I have to show your pretty friend is for her eyes only."

Then she took Inés's arm and led her to a wide bowl of water. Whispering in her ear so that her cousin wouldn't hear, she said,

"Look, *niña*. Look at the face of your husband. He's your cousin and he'll come from another place to marry you."

The vision lasted only a few moments, but Inés was captivated. She saw a face with strong features that seemed to look back at her from the surface of the water. But it was the face of a person she didn't know, and she hadn't heard of any cousin who would consider asking for her hand in marriage.

Inés and Cecilia took each other's hand to turn and run, but the old woman stood in their way with a blood-red carnation in one hand and her other hand held out, palm up.

Reflexively, or maybe out of fear of those eyes, Inés gave her a coin. Moments later, they looked for the two women in the crowd, but saw neither of them. All that was left were the bucket of carnations and the colorful gypsy tent, as though to prove that all had not been an illusion.

The fair had lost its appeal, though, and with no explanation they announced to Tutú that they wanted to go home.

That night, the cousins spoke to each other in a near whisper so as not to be heard by others, and Inés told Cecilia how the man in the water seemed to scrutinize with blue eyes that reflected the color of the sky. Neither of them could stop laughing at their own innocence, their gullibility, at how the gypsies had scared them, and at the red carnation that lay wilting on the table where they'd left it.

They never talked about their day at the fair again, and it would have been forgotten if Doctor Peralta hadn't arrived one day with an unknown and somewhat awkward young man with blond hair and eyes as blue as the sky reflected in a pool of still, clear water. The doctor introduced him as a distant relative who'd just arrived from the capital.

Three years later, Inés was walking into church on her father's arm, and as they advanced toward the altar, she remembered the words of the gypsy that afternoon at the fair, and above all the sky-blue eyes floating on the water's surface that contemplated her and attracted her irresistibly.

Years went by and the children came, one by one until there were seven. Bernardo adored Inés, but she never learned to open her heart to anyone outside the pages of a book. She had no patience with the children, and she found caring for them to be tedious and uninspiring. Fortunately, she had brought Tutú to help her, and she escaped to the library whenever possible. The scent of books still intoxicated her, and when she was immersed in their pages, she was annoyed by any distraction.

That's how I remember her. I was the sixth of the seven children that Inés brought into the world, but she paid me little heed unless I was ill. I don't remember her ever lifting me onto her lap, brushing my hair, or sharing any of those special family moments that I observed in the homes of my friends.

I'm a born rebel, and I don't bend easily to anyone else's wishes. I assert my rights and insist on having my own way. In fact, I prefer others to think as I do. All this was very displeasing to my mother, of course, who was prone to slap me or pick up the nearest object and send it flying my way when she lost her temper. I soon learned to run like a gazelle to get away from her. I would jump up onto the low roof at the back of the house and sometimes stay there for hours to avoid her, a kind of voluntary and self-imposed punishment.

Unfortunately, this mistreatment escalated, and with it my rebelliousness. Around that time, I began to ask myself why I had been born if it was to end up in this family, something I would never have wished for.

This was naïve of me, of course. Because somehow, somewhere, before I was born, an arrangement had been proposed. My spirit would be given an opportunity to inhabit a child in a difficult family, and I would more quickly recognize what was needed to overcome such challenges. The terms of this bargain must have been so harsh that I had no choice but to accept.

One day, after she gave me a particularly nasty slap and a second one was clearly imminent, I grabbed her upraised arm and told her never to hit me again, because I was not a farm animal. She must have seen in my eyes that I was serious, because she never hit me again. But physical punishment gave way to emotional abuse, which was even more painful in its own way.

My childhood was like a replay of hers, though lived under different circumstances. There were no parties for me because I wasn't given permission to go to any, because I didn't have party clothes, or simply because my mother wasn't talking to me (she subjected me to increasingly long periods of silence). I told myself that I didn't care because I didn't want to talk to her either, but this wasn't true. I didn't know why I found myself in this painful and distressing situation or how to get out of it.

Years passed, I got married, and I left home. After a while my family visits became less frequent, and we fell out of touch. Mamá died, and it took me years to understand the first task my spirit had been given. Nonetheless, the wounds had not healed. I never wanted to be a mother because I didn't want to repeat the past with my own children. I was deathly afraid that I would end up ignoring or mistreating them, because I too was prone to anger, and like my mother, I was more comfortable with books than with people.

I've had to work very hard on my image of Mamá as a mother and try to reimagine the texture of our relationship woven with threads of affection, to look beyond the aloofness that kept us apart, or to remember those rare times when our shared appreciation for a book brought us together, when we enjoyed a card game, or when she enthralled us with tales from her past.

Today I realize that behind our constant conflicts lay a strong similarity. I understand that she came to me deeply scarred by the indifference of those closest to her. She was clearly lacking in self-esteem and many other elements that enable people to value themselves and others.

To make things worse, I was born on the day after the anniversary of the death of her father and idol, Dr. Peralta, to whom she'd always compared herself and to whom she looked for affirmation. Of

24

course, she couldn't love me. My arrival at her time of mourning couldn't have been less opportune.

My self-esteem dramatically worsened when I realized that we were both victims, and that we shared a destiny. The beings who assigned her the task of being my mother were also those who would later be so satisfied to give me the task of being her daughter, because they knew it would help me grow. I learned that the key to rising above the indifference of a mother is simply to love. Love heals everything, without exception.

https://www.youtube.com/watch?v=bLHN1zEMRUM

Amor de Hombre (from the zarzuela Leyenda del Beso, by Juan Vert and Reveriano Soutullo)

My mother was my first teacher, and she was one of the most difficult challenges I've faced, but I've finally come to a place where I can put my hand over my heart and say "Thank you, Mamá. You were just what I needed."

A Lesson on Forgiveness

He'd lost all sense of time. Had it been two days, three days, or more? Trying to think gave him a headache. And his legs hurt in that scrunched up position, but he dared not move. He could still hear the voice of his *viejo*, his old man, as he walked away. That's what young Alejandro called his father, because he seemed so old. He'd told him:

"Duck in under there, son, and don't move no matter what, even if you hear me screaming. Understand? If you come out of there, I'll give you a good beating for disobeying me."

Alejandro wasn't always obedient, but he'd learned to fear the beatings that the *viejo* gave him if he took too long to bring in the bucket after milking, or if he was late in taking his father his lunch when he was out working in the fields. But that was long ago. Lately their lives had been reduced to the sound of shooting in the distance and running for cover. His brothers had left home days before, and there was no news of them. Happy to be going to war, they just said goodbye one morning and left to look for the Conservative troops, who couldn't be far away. When the fighting came to their own hill, his mother didn't hide because she couldn't leave the stove unattended. She just crossed herself and said "Jesus, Mary, and Joseph." He and his *viejo* ran to the streambank. His father had made him hide in the vegetation there before, warning him not to move so his head wouldn't stick out. And he'd always returned for him when the shooting died down. But this time, night fell and his father wasn't back.

He fell asleep despite his fear, and then he woke up cold and hungry. He hadn't had anything to eat since breakfast the day before, and although they were poor, he always had at least an *arepa* and a hot cup of *agua de panela*, water sweetened with dark loaf sugar, for breakfast. He imagined his mother grilling the arepa that she would bring his viejo in a few minutes if the shooting died down. He listened hard and was disappointed to hear firing that was sharper and closer than ever. The birds weren't even singing. He wondered if the frogs could hear the shots and looked down at the water to see what they were doing.

He didn't remember the water being that color. It looked almost red today, like the earth his father scratched out to plant the yuca that he brought to town on Sundays at harvest time. Or to plant pineapples. His mouth watered to think of those sweet pineapples looking like crowns pointing at the sky, and that took on every shade of green and yellow, and finally looked like a field of blazing torches. He'd learned when it was time to harvest the fruit, and sometimes his father let him help. If he didn't get to the field late because he was chasing crickets or shooting birds with his slingshot, that is. But he couldn't help it. Every time his mother told him to bring lunch to the old man, he swore he'd get right there. But the path was full of distractions, and come what may, he broke his promise. As a punishment, he would get a couple of lashes on his behind. This brought tears to his eyes, but he'd learned to bite his lip and take the beating, because otherwise the old man would just give him more. Then he awoke from this daydream. There'd be no pineapples to cut that day, and no possibility of seeing his viejo handle the machete expertly as he sliced the fruit from the plant. Swoosh, and the round fruit would roll down the hill until it was stopped by some bush. He loved to see those "pineapple races," as he called them! If he was lucky and the old man let him help, that is if the morning chill kept the crickets from coming out and he didn't dawdle on the way, he'd bet on how far the next pineapple would roll down the hill. And he always won.

He realized that he was daydreaming again, however, and he looked back at the water running through the bushes. It was redder, and the stream was swollen and rising. Yesterday the water reached no higher than the top of his legs, but today his underwear was soaking wet. And it was cold out.

This area around Palonegro was like that, his mother said. In the daytime, the sun's intense rays were too much to take, but at night and in the early morning you needed the heat of another body to withstand the cold. This was fine when his three brothers were there, because they all slept in one bed, but since they'd left, the nights were long. He tried in vain to warm himself up under the old *ruana*, the poncho-like woolen garment that his father didn't use any more and gave him for a blanket. Everything he had was a hand-me-down. The yuca that his father raised didn't bring in enough money to buy clothes for all of them, and since he was the youngest, his brothers gave him good clothing as they outgrew it, and his parents never needed to buy him anything. During the week, his mother mended the clothes that he wore to go to town on Sunday with his father. Alejandro was happy, even proud to have the new or almost new clothes that he wore. You had to look closely to see where his brother had torn a shirt climbing a tree or where it had caught on the barbed wire when he slid underneath the fence to chase an escaped calf. In any case, Alejandro paid no attention to where his clothes had been mended, and if he didn't see it then nobody else would either.

He looked at the water again, and he was shocked to see the first body floating downstream. He'd seen dead bodies before, when he and his old man were walking back from town a few months earlier. His father explained that there'd probably been a drunken brawl, and this bloodied man all twisted up on the ground was one of the losers. He smelled bad. That's the smell of blood, his viejo told him. Now, the water of the stream was starting to smell the same way, and he shuddered. He was sure that the water was red with blood.

As the sun rose higher, its rays grew stronger and beat down directly on his bare head. All he could do was kneel lower into the bloody water and wait. That's what his father had told him to do, and soon he'd come back for him. He began to count dead bodies to keep his mind off the hunger pangs. By then he'd seen three. Thankfully the current was steady, and there were no rocks for the bodies to get stuck against. He heard the sound of flapping wings

34

and looked up. Then he saw vultures circling above, some of them diving downward. They were going to feed on what was available. The previous year, when a goat was lost and he was told to go find it, he traipsed up and down the ridge looking fruitlessly, until vultures like these helped him find it. Unfortunately, it was too late. Four or five birds tore at the goat's skin and bones, but there was nothing else left of the animal that they'd been planning to sell in order to buy new sandals. That's why he was still barefoot. Sandals were expensive, and since his brothers completely wore theirs' out, there was nothing for him to inherit. But he had thick skin on the soles of his feet from climbing up and down the hillsides. Sometimes he got a cut or a thorn in his foot, but he'd learned which rocks were safe to step on. Round stones weren't bad, and they didn't get too hot in the sun. It was just a matter of keeping an eye out and jumping across to avoid the sharp-edged ones.

He hadn't been afraid at nightfall the night before, because he was sure his old man would be back, and he fell asleep with that thought on his mind. But today was different, and he was beginning to get scared. Hunger was keeping him awake and the night seemed very long and dark. He never knew that nights could be so long, because he'd never before been awake so late. He always went to bed as soon as they had their evening's *agua de panela*, which was such an important part of the campesino diet, along with a piece of beef jerky if they were lucky.

Thinking about food made his stomach hurt, so he decided to think about something else. He hadn't known that hunger caused pain, but his stomach felt like that time when he came upon a blackberry bush near the stone wall of their ill-tempered neighbor Anselmo. Maybe that's why he picked every last blackberry on the far side of the wall, because that old guy deserved to be left without a single one. Thankfully, don Anselmo didn't see him, because his yelling scared him even more than his old man's belt. One day, he'd chased him away and sicked his dogs on him just because he was climbing on the stone wall. But yeah, that's why he left him without a single berry. What he didn't know was that green blackberries give you stomach cramps, and since he couldn't tell anyone why his belly hurt, his mother made him drink a foul-tasting tea made out of God-knows-what bitter herb. But it worked, and the next day he didn't even remember how badly his belly had hurt. While she was making him drink the tea, his mother said that green blackberries give you cramps like the ones you had, and then raised her voice to add that "since the goat ate the blackberry bush there aren't any around here." He looked away and pretended not to hear her, but if he'd had time to go back to the fence, he would've looked for more blackberries anyway. But that lesson was good for something: Green berries, no. From now on he'd only eat ripe ones, ripe ones as red as blood...

A shiver went up his spine when he realized that dawn was coming and the sunlight would let him see the pool of blood that his hiding place had become. His old man had told him not to move for any reason in the world, but if he only had the

37

courage to disobey... No, it was better to stick it out a little longer. Today they'd come for him. But the day was slow and monotonous. The sun, the bodies, the vultures, the stench, the shadows, the sound of indistinct voices in the distance. He no longer knew how many days had passed; they were all the same, and all he could think of was his headache. He was very thirsty, and he got dizzy if he tried to move. At first, he'd taken sips of the water, but now it was dark red and smelled like rotten eggs, and when water smelled that awful, even the animals wouldn't drink it.

Something was different today, he thought. He couldn't remember when he'd last heard shooting, but the absolute silence was even more frightening than the guns and the shouting. Even the vultures were acting differently. Their stomachs were so full that they seemed to be choosing their carrion more selectively and feeding more slowly, and they weren't competing among themselves for that last bit of flesh to be torn from the bones. He felt sick to his stomach and decided that he couldn't wait for his father any longer. The viejo must have forgotten where he'd hid him. Why not, if sometimes he forgot where he put the shoulder bag with the arepas and the *guarapo*, the fermented juice that Mamá gave him in the morning? Yes, that must be it. He'd forgotten him. Why hadn't he thought of that before? Alejandro, on the other hand, hadn't forgotten the way back home. He thought he could get back by himself, and he decided to try. He dragged himself along the ground slowly so he could play dead if anyone saw him. Nobody could say that he wasn't the cleverest boy in Palonegro. Inch by inch, he left the stream behind. The sun warmed his legs, and soon he decided that if he stood up, they'd do his bidding. First, he got up on his hands and knees, and lifting his head off the ground, he could see where he was. Everything was changed, though. There were bodies lying all around him. He couldn't say how many because he didn't know how to count beyond ten, but there were more than he would have thought possible. How disgusting, he thought. Just the idea of spending another night amidst that rotting flesh led him to stand up and run.

When he got to the ridge, he saw what was left of the house: nothing but blackened walls. He was sure they were the walls of his house, but there was no roof, and there was nothing left inside, not even an arepa. There had always been at least an arepa to eat, even after he took a beating for disobeying his father. And now that he thought about it, there was no sign of his parents. He timidly approached the house, and he was convinced that he was in the right place when he found a scorched piece of his mother's apron among the ashes. But there was no sign of them. His eyes filled with tears, and when he finally wept, they streamed down his face like the water in the stream where he'd been hiding. He curled up clinging to the small piece of his mother's apron. It no longer smelled like her, only like smoke, but he fell asleep clutching it, overwhelmed with fatigue and emotion.

The next day, he scratched around in the ashes and found some pieces of dried meat where his mother always kept it wrapped in rags to keep the flies off. He had to go look for his folks before they forgot him. He went back to the stream, hoping to find his father looking for him, and he decided to follow it down the mountain because that would take him to the road into town. Soon his feet started to hurt. He knew he hadn't walked very far, but he was so weak that he didn't have the strength to go on. From time to time he saw people he didn't recognize and hid until they passed by.

It rained that night, and though he got cold, the water washed off some of the caked-on blood. The next day he came to a small puddle and felt better after drinking. He set out on the road and got to town after a few hours. Girón was deserted. Later he would find out that many of its inhabitants had fled in fear because of the shooting up in the mountains where he'd been. Others were afraid to come out of their houses unless it was necessary, and when he arrived they must have been taking their siestas. He walked aimlessly because he didn't know his way around. When he came to town on Sundays with his father, they went only to the market square. Finally he came upon the plaza that he recognized, but it was just as deserted as the rest of town. In despair, and with no idea what to do next, he sat down on the sidewalk. That's where he was when the priest came by. Actually, he would find out later that it was the priest. At first the man in the black skirt scared him a bit, but his hunger and desperation overpowered his fear. The priest said something to him that he didn't understand. Something about his name, about his clothes… Yes, he was asking his name and why he was caked with blood. But he didn't know how to answer, because he didn't know his own name. In that time hidden among the bushes, the stream had washed away his identity and maybe that of his parents. He couldn't remember their names, either. Now he was nothing but a frightened child, encrusted with the blood of those who fell at Palonegro. Never again would he be the innocent child who hunted crickets, and he would never again eat blackberries, because he associated them with the color of blood, and after he dried his eyes with the piece of his mother's apron he would never cry again, even if he wanted to.

He had to admit that the priest was patient with him. His voice came back only gradually, but finally he was able to relate how he'd felt alone at night, how he could tell from the ground that the vultures were growing fat, how he heard no birdsong or even the chirping of crickets. Yes, even the crickets left him alone, so cowardly that they fled at the first sound of shooting. But he could never describe the smell of blood. If he even tried, he felt nauseous and thought he would vomit, and he didn't want to soil Padre Hinestroza's cassock.

The padre let him curl up by the stove at night. He thought about his parents and looked forward to Sunday market day, when they would be reunited. Now that there was no more fighting up in the mountains, people had begun to drift back into town. The market had come back to life, although with far less produce because few people were left in the countryside to grow fruit and vegetables. He knew all this because on Sunday morning, the priest's cook María didn't put the pot of broth on the stove. Instead, she put on her shawl to go to the market square. There she would see what she could find to throw in the pot for the coming week, and he would follow on her heels.

At first, she ignored him. Or she began to ignore him after it was clear that the priest was not interested in her complaints. She was heard to say that the priest was off his rocker. How could he dare bring this snot-nosed kid into the house when they had practically nothing to eat? How was she going to feed him? She went on like this until she got tired of complaining and pushing him out of her way. Now she even looked for him around the house, and more than once, he'd seen her shake her head and lift up the corner of her apron as though she wanted to clean something out of her eye. This happened especially after she went to the market plaza on Sunday and saw him running around, looking everywhere for his parents, then returning home disappointed. As the weeks went by, going to the Sunday market became a routine rather than an urgent need for him. The faces of his parents and his brothers began to fade from his memory, as did their names and even his own. Since he couldn't tell Padre Hinestroza his baptismal name, the priest gave him the name Alejandro, like the great Greek conqueror. Nobody knows what the clergyman meant by giving him this name, or if he meant anything at all by it.

When the padre wasn't celebrating the Latin mass, he sat on the patio in the shade of a mango tree to read his threadbare books. He read the same books over and over again, he told Alejandro, because books weren't easy to come by. It's not like he talked much to the boy, though. Other than giving him a place to sleep and seeing that he didn't go hungry—which luckily wasn't a problem because the parishioners all came to mass with a little something for the parish house—Alejandro was like one more piece of furniture in the household. Nobody paid much attention to what he did, even to scold him, so he had plenty of time to roam around town. He just had to remember to be back for meals, because Señora María would be furious if he let them get cold. And he mustn't miss the afternoon Rosary. Other than this, he had the whole day to wander around town. Being naturally curious, he had begun to go into abandoned houses and scrape around in the patios. One afternoon, he heard someone say that those who fled the fighting had left their savings hidden in copper containers. Despite his best efforts, though, he never found any treasure.

After a while, he began to linger at the Sunday market after María finished shopping and was ready to leave. At first he carried people's purchases for them, but then he began to take on heavier loads, and although the tips were small, he always came home with some change to add to his own treasure, which he kept wrapped in a handkerchief stashed behind a loose stone on the patio. In addition to these coins, he had the strip of his mother's apron and a piece of charred wood that reminded him of his house, or what had been left of it. He lacked for nothing, since someone always left him an old shirt or pair of pants at the church. Nobody gave him any overt love or affection, but if he followed the rules and behaved himself, someone might smile at him, tousle his hair, or pat him on the back, and María would give him an extra square of butter if there was one to be had.

He no longer remembered how many years he'd been there. The inertia of the town had taken hold of his soul the day he arrived. Or maybe he'd left his soul in the stream or the road down from the mountain into Girón. Yes, that must be it, because while he remembered dragging it along the road as he tripped over rocks and avoided brambles, he was never conscious of it again. Whatever small piece of his soul that was left must have broken off in his first days at the padre's house, because all that sustained him was waiting for the next Sunday. But not even that wasn't enough anymore.

One day he heard an ominous cough, and soon the padre was coughing frequently. When he sat under the leaves of the mango tree, he wore a shawl across his shoulders, but he shivered nonetheless. Even on hot days, he avoided the shade of the tree and preferred to sit in his office listening to the monotonous ticking of the clock, with barely enough strength to turn the pages of a book. Alejandro watched the priest from a corner of the room, and it broke his heart to see him suffer so.

On the Sunday after Easter, the padre didn't get up for mass, and María swatted Alejandro on the head for running into the kitchen.

"Hush," she said. "Can't you see the padre needs to rest? When will you learn not to make so much noise?"

From that day on, he glided along the walls hoping to dissolve into his shadow, a shadow that wouldn't make a sound and cause him an undeserved scolding. He tried to walk without touching the floor, and to hold his breath lest his respiration be too loud. Only the beating of his heart betrayed him. He slept under the overhang of the patio because he'd outgrown his corner of the kitchen, but now he lay awake at night gnawing on his knuckles and wondering what would happen next.

He'd heard María whispering with Señora Remedios, a neighbor with tight gray braids who looked as old as the hills, and the Señora said that her father had died from the same cough. María crossed herself and Alejandro understood from her expression that she expected the worst. On another day, a neighbor from around the corner who kept goats also came by, supposedly to bring the padre some of the candy she made, but she was such a gossip that he knew she was really there to see what first-hand information she could share the next day in the park where she and others gathered under the ceiba tree.

Before leaving with the latest juicy gossip, she casually mentioned that Argemiro from the store had told her that his compadre in Bucaramanga told him that a replacement for Padre Hinestroza was already lined up. Alejandro didn't really know what that meant, but something inside told him that the padre was not long for this world and his own life in Girón was not going to last much longer.

And so it was. A few days later, he found doña María crying inconsolably in the kitchen, and he didn't need to ask what was wrong. He turned without a word and went to his corner of the patio, where he removed the loose stone and took out his little bundle. He didn't look back at the house and he didn't say goodbye. Why should he? He'd learned that it was better to disappear without a trace, like his parents and his brothers. María would soon forget about him, too. Anyway, what would he say to her? Hardened as he was, he wouldn't be one to express gratitude, and it would never even occur to him to give her a hug. Where he was from, boys were taught to be macho, not to go around hugging people. His old man had never hugged him, as far as he could remember. Nor his mother. If anything, they might give him an extra mouthful of sweet roll if he got bruised or didn't feel well. So he shrugged, took a deep breath, and stepped out onto the street.

By this time, the town was waking up for the morning. He saw a woman sweeping her sidewalk and he heard a baby crying in the house at the corner. He crossed paths with don Remigio, who was coming back from milking the cows he kept across the bridge on the road out of town. It was a normal day, and no one was surprised to see Alejandro walking through town toward the road to Bucaramanga. In fact, nobody paid him any attention. They were completely accustomed to seeing the snot-nosed kid that the padre had taken in. Nobody greeted him when he got to Girón several years before, and nobody said goodbye when he left. He didn't have a lot more now than when he'd arrived, and he was just a few years older. But how old was he? When he got to town he was losing his last baby teeth, but that was some time ago. Now he could feel whiskers sprouting on his smooth face, and María said his voice was changing. On the few occasions when she looked at him, she made comments such as "you'll have to shave soon," or "just look how the hair is sprouting on your chest." This was true, so he tried to throw water on his body early in the morning, before she came out on the patio to dump her chamber pot and that of the padre. But these were the only clues

51

to his age, which he had no way to calculate. In any case, he'd had a lifetime's worth of experience in a relatively short time.

That's why he wasn't afraid when he set out walking to Bucaramanga. He didn't look back even once, and he didn't stop until he'd walked a good part of the eight kilometers between the two towns. He drank from the river and even bathed along the way, giving him a chance to hide his savings. Since he didn't have a belt, he tied the bundle to his waist and covered it with his shirt as he tucked it into his trousers.

He buttoned his long-sleeved shirt right up to the neck that day, a habit that would be second nature to him throughout his life. He didn't want anyone to see the hair on his chest or for anyone to joke about how white his skin was. He realized that day that he would need a sombrero to look older. All adult men used sombreros, and he was a man now. By the time he was on the last hill before entering Bucaramanga, he'd decided to buy himself one at the market. He didn't know when market day was in this city, though, and he had to begin by locating the market plaza. But this wasn't hard. After spending years on the streets of Girón, he knew how to observe people's behavior. It took him no time at all to tell which of them were coming into town to buy or sell at the plaza, so he just followed them. And just as in Girón, nobody paid him any attention.

Compared to Girón, Bucaramanga was a bustling city. Everyone was in a hurry, and if he hadn't reacted so quickly, he would have been trampled by a man on horseback the first time he turned a corner. After that scare, he decided to rest on the sidewalk, which gave him a few minutes to study his surroundings. The market square was emptying out, and the people who were leaving carried baskets and shoulder bags. Some of them paid a young guy with a cart to carry their purchases home. The most prosperous of them hired mules, and some women, probably household servants, were followed home by porters carrying heavy baskets secured by a strap around their foreheads.

After all the others had gone, only the vendors were left at the market. They were sweeping up, washing their stalls, and bagging garbage. Hoping to find something to eat, he stepped into the plaza and began helping to move boxes, take down awnings, and clean up. Suddenly his eagle eyes spotted a movement on the ground, a rat's tail behind a sack of long-stemmed onions. Without a thought he grabbed it and slammed the animal against the ground, killing it. The sound attracted the attention of a vendor, who laughed out loud, and without missing a beat, passed Alejandro a gourd of *guarapo* and a broom.

Alejandro helped the vendor until his market stall was tidy and clean, and when the man said good evening to Alejandro, he casually said that he'd expect him the next day; by coincidence he'd dismissed his delivery boy. It was an easy decision for Alejandro to agree to this proposal. He hadn't eaten anything that day except for a few scraps that people had dropped or thrown away, and he was hungry again that night.

He was plagued with painful memories, but he found a place to sleep in a park, and when the church bell struck three, he made his way to the market. This would be his routine for a time. The vendor was a good man, always smiling and going out of his way to help others. If someone asked for a product that was sold out, he'd send Alejandro to another stall to find it for them. Alejandro was good at this, and he always got a small tip if he brought it back quickly. He didn't earn much, but customers gave him a coin from time to time, and he was provided with an afternoon meal.

In any case, Alejandro had ambition. He hoped to at least be able to buy the sombrero and espadrilles he longed for. At his age, it was time to have both these things. So, on days when there was no market, he walked around town and paid close attention to everything going on around him. On one of these days, he heard people talking about *aguadores*. Since he didn't know this word, he stopped to hear what they were saying. It turned out that aguadores were men who transported spring water to town after collecting it at a place called Chorreras de don Juan. They used burros, it was said, and they had an increasing number of clients. This was very interesting. Most people in Bucaramanga got their water from small wells, of which there were many. But these wells did not provide a great deal of water, and more prosperous people preferred to have water delivered. Unfortunately, thought Alejandro, you needed money to get a donkey. If it weren't for that, he could work as an aguador in the afternoons after the market closed.

He kept his ears open from that moment on, and an opportunity was not long in coming. An unknown disease was raging through Bucaramanga, and while many were afflicted, many more were shaken and fearful. The doctors in town would need more clean water, he thought, and he set out to find himself a burro. Fortune smiled on him on the third day of his search. Someone mentioned in the market plaza that a donkey was being sold because its owner had died and his widow needed cash for the burial. Alejandro retrieved his "hidden treasure," as he called it, and counted his savings. He needed a *burro*, even if that meant he couldn't afford a new sombrero.

The widow greeted him with something between gratitude and resignation. She'd wanted more than what this kid was offering, but it had already been two days since her husband died, and unless she found a way to pay for a decent burial, she'd have no choice but to bury him in a pauper's grave.

That wouldn't do. Ramiro had been a good husband and he deserved at least a minimally decent burial. In any case, she'd also need a grave marker to visit weekly to tell him how she was and what the kids were doing, how they were getting on now that he was gone. So she accepted what Alejandro offered her and bid the burro farewell. The animal would be better off in other hands, anyway, since she didn't have money for its feed.

So Alejandro got his burro, and from one day to the next he joined the aqueduct of the three b's, as it was known: burro, barrel, and *bobo*, or simpleton.

His plan to haul water only in the afternoons fell by the wayside. On the first day that he went to the Chorreras de don Juan for water, he realized that it would be better to start early, because the clients wanted fresh water in the morning to start the day.

Alejandro had no regrets, and he wasn't nostalgic. He hadn't looked back when he left Girón, and he didn't look back when he left the market plaza. Alejandro the errand boy died that day; now he was Alejandro the *aguador*, and he would have the best clients.

Lucky for him, he already knew the city like the back of his hand. In particular, he knew where the doctors lived, especially a doctor newly arrived from the capital whom he saw walking to his office every day, and who'd acknowledged him with a slight wave of the hand on more than one occasion as they crossed the street. So, once he filled his barrels, he headed over to Dr. Peralta's house, where his loud confrontation with the "bureaucracy" at the door eventually led the doctor himself to emerge from his study, as Alejandro had intended.

The domestics were accustomed to purchasing water daily, but he wanted them to understand that he wasn't looking for daily sales, but a "contract." The more he insisted, however, the more they remonstrated with him and threatened to shut the door in his face. The doctor was trying to study inside, but this commotion at the front door made it impossible. When he came out to intervene, he found himself face to face with a squalid youngster, a half-starved burro, and leaky barrels of water. Dr. Peralta found the overall image so evocative that it suggested a scene from Don Quixote. The young women were poking at the lad, who in turn refused to give an inch. Then the burro snorted. Dr. Peralta almost burst out laughing, but he remembered his elevated status as a medical doctor and thought it would seem disrespectful for him to make light of his domestic employees. He managed to keep a straight face and asked what was going on. Alejandro explained his preference for a contract, and the doctor settled the matter by saying that if the water was delivered every morning before eight o'clock, he'd have had no problem paying a monthly fee.

The domestics looked at each other with great surprise. Alejandro wanted to jump and shout, but something in the doctor's face told him that this would not be appropriate, so he nodded gravely, took up the burro's halter in a businesslike fashion, and sauntered importantly down the street, oblivious to the chortles of the young women standing at the door.

He, Alejandro Hinestroza, was now the *aguador* to the house of Dr. Peralta. He didn't care if they called him a *bobo*, or if they scoffed at his old gray donkey. It didn't matter that his barrels were ancient, and least of all that he didn't have frayed espadrilles or even a raggedy sombrero. But they would see... things would change, and everything would be better from this day on.

❧

Alejandro told me all this and much more. My first memories of him coincide with my first days at school. While Alejandro was a constant presence in my house, I'd never talked to him. Always taciturn, he arrived in the afternoon wearing a long-sleeved white shirt buttoned to the neck, khaki pants, a gray felt sombrero, and carrying a staff. And of course, he wore impeccable white espadrilles with soles made of tires, fastened around his ankle with a black strap. One ankle had the marks of a thousand mosquito bites, and his leathery heels revealed that he'd walked barefoot for long distances on many a day. Alejandro was old by then. To my five-year-old eyes he seemed ancient, and his faraway gaze earned my respect.

When I started school, I would sit on a wall in front of the house to wait for the bus, and Alejandro would show up after lunch to sit a few meters away, always serious and respectful. Day after day he'd greet me, tip his hat politely, and sit down on the wall. This was fitting for a man who luxuriated in his retirement after many years of hard work.

Little by little, we broke the ice. I got up the nerve to ask him questions and he would respond if he had an answer. Sometimes I showed him my notebooks, and I saw the delight in his eyes. He never learned to write, he said. He'd started working at a very young age.

Occasionally, the seamstress of the house waited for him with a full needle cushion and a spool of thread. Even though he was over 60, he could see better than her without needing glasses, and he had a reputation among the seamstresses of the town as the person most skilled at threading needles. This greatly impressed me as a reason to be proud. The best needle threader worked at my house, I would boast to my classmates. They would open their eyes wide but say nothing. Now I understand that they didn't even have needle threaders at home, let alone the best in town.

Alejandro was silent as he carried out his assigned task. He would furrow his brow and concentrate on threading one needle after the other. The bus arrived for me, and I climbed on board, frustrated because I hadn't been able to talk to him that day.

Sometimes he disappeared for long periods, and when I was a little older I realized that his frame of mind was cyclical. He'd disappear whenever elections were coming up. He was born into a Conservative family and the Liberals had made his life a living hell, so it would be better if he weren't seen at our house, "so they wouldn't do away with him once and for all." "Who knows, they might even poison me." "Anyway," he said loudly so my mother would hear from inside, "in Conservative houses they take care of me and feed me well. Who needs these Liberals, anyway? May God strike them dead." More than once, he accomplished his goal of antagonizing Mamá. She would burst out the door roaring that she had no need for ingrates in her house.

I never really learned how my mother had inherited him. As Dr. Peralta's only daughter, she'd inherited his intelligence, his discerning nature, his house, and his jewelry. But along with many and diverse other human specimens, she also inherited Alejandro and took responsibility for his well-being. I can't say anything about the period after Alejandro first brought water to my grandfather's house in about 1911, and up to 1960. Nor do I know anything about his participation in the mid-century conflict between the political parties universally known as "the Violence," or how he survived that strange and tragic episode. What I do know is that my mother kept her promise up to the day of his death. She saw to it that Alejandro never wanted for a plate of food or a roof over his head. It's true that he never slept in our house. That would be more than a Conservative like him could tolerate, but Mamá always paid for his room nearby.

I bothered Alejandro with many simple questions, and he began to get over his shyness with me. When he was in a good mood, he would tell me about his life, until he came to certain distressing details, that is. Then his sky-blue eyes would darken.

He would straighten himself up, pull down the brim of his sombrero, and say that he had to get going because he had much to do. This was not true, of course, because his only occupation by that time was to wander around town. From the time of his childhood, he never lost his enthusiasm for observing all that was to be seen on the streets, and as he grew older, he also began to collect amulets.

One day he showed me some colored pencils that he had in the shoulder bag he'd begun to carry. On another day I saw a piece of cardstock jutting out of the bag, and I asked to see it. It was a full-page drawing of a wall made of black and purple stones. On the next day, he had another one with more stones, and the following day many more. He drew nothing but stones. High stone walls, almost always black, purple, or blue, with only an occasional splash of yellow.

Sometimes he was so proud of his artwork that he'd hand me his daily drawing without a word. Even though I found the walls suffocating and I would never have hung his work, it was touching to see him draw them. He concentrated so hard while he worked that he seemed to hold his breath. At the same time, he bit down on his tongue where it peeked out of the corner of his mouth. Sometimes he'd remove his hat and lay it by his side. Then I got to see more of his hair, which by this time was almost all white. But he didn't like to be seen hatless, and his impulsive act of taking it off when he was focused on his work was corrected with a more considered action, replacing it before too much time had passed. He was likewise uncomfortable being seen with dirty clothes or even with the top button of his shirt open.

Many years later he became incontinent, and at times he arrived with a dark wet stain on his pants reaching from his groin to his knee. I don't think he was even aware of these things by then, however, because he never stopped bringing me his drawing of the day. Sometimes he drew day and night, while at other times he was happy just staring off into the distance and speaking in a low voice, almost to himself…

"You know what, *mi niña*? I don't even remember my parents anymore. I got tired of looking for my brothers, too. I used to ask everyone who'd been in the war if they'd heard anything about José or Jesús Moro."

"Moro?" I interrupted, "what do you mean? Didn't you tell me your family name was Hinestroza?"

"Oh, *mi niña*, don't confuse me. I've always been Alejandro Hinestroza de Peralta. Let me talk and stop interrupting me. My brothers' name was Moro."

"But Alejandro," I said, contradicting him again despite his remonstrances, "if your brothers' name was Moro, then yours is, too."

I'd offended him, and he got up and walked off without a word. I knew then that he would stop coming to the house for a while.

But he always came back. After the elections, he'd reappear like a child after being scolded, meek as could be—for a while, at least. Mamá didn't look

67

at him, nor did the cook, my nanny, or especially Papá, who always looked through him anyway. After a few days, someone would get up the nerve to tell him that his last outburst was the height of disrespect, and he'd smile mischievously. Then everything would go back to normal.

After Alejandro died, I tried to find out more about him, but Mamá didn't know much more, and she just repeated the same things he'd been telling me since he came to my grandfather's house. People who hadn't known him when he was young called him "*el bobo* Alejandro," Alejandro the simpleton. Others called him "old man Alejandro." I heard them say these things, but I knew that he'd always be simply Alejandro to me.

When Alejandro finally died, he was over 90. I don't remember where he was buried or whether his grave was marked with a stone, a cross, an epitaph, or even his name. "Alejandro was a good *bobo*," my mother told me one day. "And he knew how to make poetry out of stones," I added.

https://www.youtube.com/watch?v=SoR8KxPD_60

Pueblito viejo (José A. Morales) and more.

There are two opposing forces in Alejandro's life story. The first was a remarkable resilience that enabled him to come to terms with adversity and adjust to circumstances. When I find myself at an impasse and feel that the world may be just too much to handle, I think back on my memories of him. Using my spiritual resources, I call upon some of what I learned from Alejandro, and like magic, I find a solution. He was one of my first life-teachers, and I am eternally grateful for everything he imparted to me.

That's why I never understood his other, dark side, the part that wouldn't release him from his hatred for the opposing side in the violent conflict of his early days, the War of a Thousand Days. His inability to forgive. Until my brother Roberto was kidnapped, that is.

My phone rang very early, at four in the morning, and the news could not have been more devastating. (Funny thing, bad news often comes before the waking hour, and the sudden interruption of our REM sleep leaves us disoriented and leads to heart palpitations).

The kidnapping lasted three months and ten days. It's an experience that tore us apart in a way that I wouldn't wish on any family. The fragile threads that held us together disintegrated, supplanted by deep divisions that even time has never fully reconciled.

One might think that the kidnapping of a loved one is over when they return, but nobody can prepare themself for what comes next. Roberto came home, but an important part of him, including all that was good, never returned from the jungle where he was held. He had become an angry, bitter, and resentful person, which was truly painful to all who knew him.

We had been very close before his kidnapping, united in our sorrow at the death of his daughter (described below). But suddenly it seemed that I barely knew him. He spoke so hatefully of his captors that he drained me of all energy and left me exhausted. At first I thought it was a phase that he would soon leave behind, but that was not to be.

Years later, when a peace agreement was signed with the guerrillas, it was too much for him, and his heart simply stopped beating. The doctors said it was a heart attack, but no, it was the hate that consumed him and finally broke his heart.

I'm grateful to Roberto for many things. He believed in me when no one else did, and he reached out to me on many occasions when I was overwhelmed by my problems with our mother. He taught me many things, including the art of carpentry.

Above all, both he and Alejandro set examples that taught me not to hate. It's interesting that, as in this case, we can learn from both positive and negative examples. I can say that thanks to them, I renounced rancor and eliminated the word hate from my vocabulary. If any such feelings tempt me, I say "No thank you, I choose to forgive." Forgiveness is liberating, and it's a balm for the soul. If a person hurts you, it's their problem, not yours. We're in this world to be happy and share love. Don't let anyone turn you away from these guiding principles.

Unconditional Love

"Are you sleeping yet, kids?" Tutú's voice was drowsy, and we tried to imitate her with a somnolent "Yes." Then we'd wait 'til she left the room and continue our conversation. It's not that our conversations were very long or meaningful, but it made us feel important to break a rule as momentous as going to sleep early.

I never confessed to Bernardo that it terrified me to open my eyes and see the dim light filtering in through the high window in the room where we slept with our sister Tino, who would be sleeping soundly by then. That's why I preferred to continue talking with my eyes squeezed tightly closed. I'm not sure, but that faint light may have reminded me of the measles we'd gotten over a few days before. Our headaches were so painful that they put red tissue paper over the window, supposedly so we our skin wouldn't break out as much and the light wouldn't hurt our eyes. But the reddish half-light was the same by day and by night, and it was terrifying. My only consolation was that Tutú would come in to feel our foreheads. She had the calloused hands of a woman who'd worked from a young age, yet they felt smooth, tender, and loving. That's why the measles were short lived, but I insisted on keeping my eyes closed after she turned out the light in the evening.

Poor Tutú never found out that the bedtime stories she told us put her to sleep before us, nor that Bernardo turned his head just before the spoonsful of soup entered his mouth and let Mamá's German shepherd Califa eat it. Tutú's vision was not the best by that time, and besides, she was always distracted by her constant praying. Califa, in fact, was quite adept at drinking soup from a spoon and stealing butter from the table without disturbing the tablecloth. At least she was good for something. But that was later, in the "upper house." I shouldn't get ahead of myself.

I don't have many other memories of the "lower house," as we called the house where we lived downtown, just fragments that my brothers and I embellish when get together and share family anecdotes. It was a big house, full of extremely high-ceilinged rooms. I was so short that I couldn't reach the doorknobs, even on tippy-toe, so I could only enter rooms if they were already open. In any case, my favorite place to go was a small room where the domestics ironed, which was upstairs next to the terrace. I loved to climb into the basket of clean clothing, so big that it was like being in a dollhouse. And I'd stay there until one of the women ordered me out, scolding me because I had soiled this or that piece of clothing with my dirty feet. It's true that my feet must've been dirty because I hated wearing shoes and was constantly barefoot. In any case, Tutú bathed me every day and always made sure that I had clean clothes to wear and a spare set if I needed it.

She'd learned that from her mother, Delfina. Delfina was poor, Tutú would tell me, but her children always had clean clothes.

"Oh yes, Tutú, tell me more about when you were little."

"Oh, that was many years ago, *niña*." Tutú never called me by my name; I was always "la niña" or "mi niña." "Some things I don't even remember, or maybe I don't want to remember."

"Have I told you what games my brothers and I played? No? Well, while my mother cleaned house and made lunch for my father, we'd go to the swimming hole. That was when we lived in Barichara. You remember that I told you about this, right? We loved the water and we learned to swim alone, though it scared Mercedes a little bit. Don't be making that face, niña. Mercedes was my older sister; I've told you that before also. My younger brother José, on the other hand, wasn't afraid even to jump in from the highest rock. He swam like a fish, mi niña. He was like a little tadpole."

"Where's José, Tutú? How come he's never come to visit you?"

Tutú was silent for what seemed like a long time, and when she finally answered, she had a lump in her throat and spoke in a near-whisper.

"When the swimming hole dried up in the summer, we'd entertain ourselves climbing guava trees and eating ripe guava fruit. Until the accident, that is."

"What accident, Tutú?" And she fell silent. This was one of the things she didn't like to talk about. She ran an open hand over her eyes, and with the other hand she reached into her pocket for a rosary. I got bored waiting for the rest of the story and went to play somewhere else.

A few days later I was asking questions again. She complained jokingly about being "interrogated," but always with a smile, because as much as she grumbled about it, she actually loved telling stories, almost as much as I liked hearing them.

"How old was José when he had the accident? As old as me?" And I held up several fingers.

"I don't know, mi niña. Maybe 6 or 7. He was very young, and so was I. He was barely older than me."

"And what happened to him? Tell me, tell me," I repeated.

Not long after that, she finally told me more or less the whole story. They'd gone to eat guavas as they always did, but there were very few fruit left on the tree where José was climbing. He wasn't about to give up, though, so he stretched more than usual to reach a tantalizing guava just beyond his reach. He lost his balance, then he lost his footing, and by the time Tutú realized what had happened, she saw him splayed on the ground, as motionless as a rag doll. His lifeless body was surrounded by guava leaves, half-rotten fruit, and silence, utter silence. Tutú hesitated a few moments before reacting. Then she ran up the hill wailing, but by that time her mother was charging down from the house, alerted to what had happened by the bellowing of

Mercedes, who had seen everything from where she was standing next to the house. She didn't remember what happened next, just the chill that ran down her spine when the neighbors arrived with a coffin, and the procession to the cemetery with constant low-pitched sobbing punctuated by piercing wails. She never ate another guava, and we were told not to eat them because they were full of worms, like the worms she saw when she closed her eyes and imagined José there alone in the black hole where they had lowered his casket. Her childhood innocence perished on that day. It was interred in that same hole, or another like it. What does it matter? Any hole in the ground would be just as cold and dark at night.

"And your Papá? Where was he? Wasn't he at the funeral?"

"No, niña." We were in dire straits, and he'd left a long time before to look for work as a muleteer or whatever he could find. Then a few months after José's death a stranger came to town asking around for my mother, and he gave her my father's belongings: a pair of dirty, worn-out espadrilles, a stretched-out pouch, a cracked drinking gourd, and some odds and ends that must have been in his pockets. This unknown man spoke very softly to her. He had his hat pulled down low over his eyes, and said goodbye very quickly. When my mother turned back to where Mercedes and I were standing together holding hands, all we could see was that her face was as white as a sheet. She didn't cry and made no attempt to explain what had just occurred. It was like we weren't even there. But that night we heard her sobbing into her pillow, and when we got up the next morning, we found a bundle at the door. We looked in it without asking permission, and we found that she'd put all my papá's clothes in there, clean and neatly folded. After breakfast, we went out to do errands, and the bundle was gone. She never mentioned my father again. The next time my godfather came to town, he told us what had happened.

"Your godfather, Tutú? Who was that?"

"Shhh… you've made me talk a lot already. Now go to sleep and I'll tell you the rest some other day." But she never did tell us the rest.

Tutú prayed a lot. *Hail Mary, full of grace…* and her voice fell to a steady murmur. One rosary ran into the next, and although you couldn't make out the words, her lips were moving at all hours. It made no difference whether she was cooking, tending lovingly to the plants and herbs, walking the baby, or seated on a stool resting. She had a prayer for every occasion, and while she still had her health, she never failed to attend mass every day of the year. One day she told me that it was time for me to pray to the *Niño Dios*, the Christ Child, knowing that she would have to explain to me exactly who this baby was and how he was different from other babies, because I always said he looked like the baby across the street.

"Holy guardian angel, my sweet companion, forsake me not by night or by day..." I must confess that I liked the prayer up to that point, but less so when it went on to say *"leave me not alone or I shall die."* José wasn't

82

alone when he died, and I didn't die when I was alone for the whole afternoon because Tutú went to the cemetery to put flowers on her mother's grave. The next night, I closed my eyes and clasped my hands tightly over my heart to repeat the prayer. But I found myself asking the Niño Dios to never, ever take Tutú away from me, because I couldn't imagine life without her, her stories, and her affection. From then on, I held her against me as though I wanted to hug her, but really I just wanted to make sure her heart was still beating and she was still alive. I also loved how she smelled, like clean clothes dried in the sunlight after being washed with homemade soap—the same soap she used to wash her hair in the laundry room—and like the chamomile water that she used to rinse off. I loved watching her wash and comb her hair, no longer as abundant as it had once been, but with traces of the color that it had in her youth. Her hair was blonde, almost ashen, and she left it loose only when it was wet. Then she would gather it into a low bun, always held in place at her neck with two ornamental combs, like banderillas positioned by an adept torero. But what

I liked best were her eyes. No one anywhere had eyes like hers. Not even my dolls had eyes that color. They seemed to be blue, but they weren't. They were violet with undertones of different shades that came out depending on the light. Sometimes they seemed almost green, sometimes gray. One time I saw a photograph of Liz Taylor in one of my mother's magazines, and I ran to show her that Liz's eyes were so much like hers. But then I realized they were quite different. Nobody had eyes like Tutú's and I've never met anyone whose eyes were even close. She was very white, of course. At that time it never even occurred to me that there could be other skin tones. In Santander there were lots of blond, pink-skinned and blue-eyed children. From time to time, I found myself looking in the mirror and wondering why I didn't have blonde hair like my father, like Bernardo, or like the baby.

Tutú noticed, and she told me, "Your hair is pretty, mi niña. It's a little rebellious, but with this rosemary water we can tame it and make it shine.

Hold still and don't make that face because I don't want to get your clothes wet."

I held still for her, and I agreed to accompany her to the garden to pick some sprigs of rosemary. I knew that if she picked more than she needed, she would put some into my underwear drawer, which always smelled of the herb.

"You see, mi niña? The Virgin Mary always put the Christ Child's diapers out to dry on top of a rosemary bush, so he always smelled like you."

I guess I was supposed to be honored, but I stopped listening once I heard the word "diapers" because I was a big girl and didn't use them anymore. Then I made a face and went to look for Bernardo to see what kind of trouble we could cook up that day.

By then we were at the "upper house." We'd moved there soon before the baby was born. The house was enormous, and the garden was a magical place where we spent hours exploring and making discoveries. The days weren't long enough for all our games there, which included running, climbing trees, and doing somersaults. This went on until one of us landed in a nasty little treat that a dog had left the night before and the gardener had missed when he cleaned up in the morning. Tutú would clean off whichever one of us was stinky and immerse them in a washtub. But that would put an end to our garden play for the day and we'd have to find another form of entertainment.

With so much to do in the garden, I had less quality time with Tutú. Now I could only watch her as she did housework or see her when I was sick and she brought me food, saying "get better soon, mi niña. Look how skinny you are, and those are bags under your eyes. Drink this *caspiroleta*." Simply put, caspiroleta was hot eggnog. (For Christmas we drank chilled eggnog, which we call sabajón). It was nothing but milk, a raw egg, sugar, and cinnamon, but when you're coughing and feverish, the thick drink just makes you cough more and sweat like an ice cube melting in the sun. I would have preferred *Pony Malta*, a sweet, carbonated malt drink. Finally,

Tutú realized that Pony Malta was better at helping me get well, and she left bottles of it under the bed where I could reach it if she wasn't nearby to bring me one. She came into the room frequently to check on me, and if I was sleeping, she would tiptoe back out. If I was awake, though, she would look at me knowingly as though to confirm our secret, and then turn on the radio. Together we listened to Renzo the Gypsy, my first love. Yes, I fell hopelessly in love with Renzo when I was four years old, and my heart nearly burst when he spoke the name Myosotis, which was what he called his beloved Adriana, in that husky and passionate voice of his. I don't know how I managed to convince everyone to name the new baby Adriana, but somehow I did. In my heart, however, she was always Myosotis. My romance with Renzo ended when I realized that I was not the Myosotis of his dreams, and I think I lost all interest in soap operas that day. But I still liked listening to the radio. Later there was "The Fantastic School of doña Rita," which came on just as the school buses full of children passed by the house. I tried to imagine which of the students on the radio show was most like me. There was Cucúrbita Pepo, Pantaleón León, Anicete Calvete, and others whose names I don't remember, but they gave me a great deal of unforgettable fun and entertainment. "Eber Castro, the Giant of Humor" came on at noon and told very funny jokes in a Cuban accent. Then there was "Montecristo." That was more or less when Tutú came back to my room after the afternoon meal, and we laughed together listening to all the characters, such as Montecrispín, Montecrispeta, Montecristina, Montoño, and Montecristico, all of them portrayed with the voice of Guillermo Zuluaga, known as Montecristo. Or simply Monte, as he was known to his friends, including Tutú and me. After laughing 'til my belly hurt, I curled up in bed to take my siesta, while Tutú left to do her many chores.

Despite her age and having raised all the children in the house from Mamá on down, Tutú always found time to cook, starch and iron the clothing, care for the herb garden, and pray. Praying, of course was her favorite activity.

All the religious holidays had their own prayers. On the Feast of the Sacred Heart of Jesus, she could be heard praying in an undertone throughout the day:

Soul of Christ, sanctify me

Body of Christ, save meBlood of Christ, inebriate me

Water from the side of Christ, wash me

Passion of Christ, strengthen me

O good Jesus, hear me

Within Thy wounds, hide me

Separated from Thee let me never be

From the malignant enemy, defend me

At the hour of death, call me

To come to Thee, bid me

That I may praise Thee in the company of Thy Saints

for all eternity. Amen.

I was already contrary at that tender age, and I was struck by the idea of a "malignant enemy." It was hard for me to believe that we had any *good* enemies. Strangely enough, I still wonder about this, and it's still hard for me to trust a person who has been hostile but then apologizes profusely. Tutú always told me to do the right thing no matter who I was dealing with, and I don't doubt the wisdom of her advice, but if a person does wrong by me, I see them very differently. They become one of my enemies, and I look for help to defend myself from them because I can't do it on my own.

Sometimes on Good Friday, she took me to visit religious likenesses in multiple churches, but to be honest I always tried to get out of going. Even though I knew that the effigies of Christ's bloody corpse in glass-topped coffins weren't real, they always turned my stomach. Tutú would kneel before each image and pray from the bottom of her heart: *My sacramental Jesus, my sweet love and comfort, who would love you so much that they would die of love?*

The smell of incense, the smoky candles, the hot breath of parishioners beating their chests in mourning with their black-shawled heads inclined toward effigies of suffering, the black bunting hung over other images in the church, the murmur of a thousand voices like swarms of bees buzzing around our heads: It all made me want to run away, and I couldn't wait to see her beat her chest for the last time, make the sign of the cross, and laboriously straighten herself up... I have to confess that this was my least favorite part of Holy Week. I loved the processions on the other days, and my heart would skip a beat when each new float rolled into view, but there were no processions on Good Friday, only those interminable prayers to the bloodied Christ.

I held her hand tightly all the way home. It was my anchor to terra firma after navigating those turbulent seas of supplication and murmuration. Holding her hand, I walked along wordlessly and oblivious to our surroundings. It took me the rest of the day for the full weight of those church visits to dissipate, while as soon as Tutú walked in the door and took off her shawl, she went purposefully to the kitchen and the earthenware crock where she was preparing the beverage known as *masato,* made of ground rice, syrup, and spices. Her masato was like no other. She mixed it constantly, added ingredients, and mixed it again. Nothing she produced in the kitchen, including her masato, was based on a simple recipe. In fact, it seemed to entail a days-long ritual.

As soon as I heard Tutú ask the gardener to bring her the earthenware crock, I prepared myself for what was coming. I loved being by her side while she washed it thoroughly and left it to air out in the sunlight for a couple of days, then inspected it meticulously, making sure that it smelled just right. I held my breath until she nodded her approval and placed it in a corner where it would be protected from the breeze.

The masato needs to rest, she told me. It can't be made where everyone comes by, or it will get bitter. She prepared a strong *agua de panela*, the beverage made from loaf sugar, and dumped it into the crock, immediately covering the container with a clean cloth and a plate to hold it down. A week later, she discarded the agua de panela, which was no longer clear and sweet, but cloudy, sedimented, and strong smelling. She repeated this operation, and when the day to prepare the masato finally arrived, she rinsed out the crock with freshly boiled water and declared her satisfaction with its readiness for the procedure.

If you don't do this, she told me, the masato will smell of soap and be tainted by all the crud that soaks into the pores of the crock while it's in storage. Naturally, I agreed. I was convinced that there was no greater wisdom than hers.

Then she cooked rice, ground it, and put it through a fine sieve. She expertly kneaded the cooked rice and the netting of the sieve so the grain disappeared little by little into the waiting crock. Next, she added the syrup that she had made with cinnamon and cloves, and replaced the cloth that covered the crock. That was the end of phase one. Three days later, she uncovered the mix, gave us a taste of it, and added more syrup if it was too thick or more rice if it was too thin. Occasionally she'd add both to increase its volume. Now the masato was ready, and all that was left was to keep the crock full. I'll never forget the smell of the masato, the bubbles that clung to the sides of our drinking glasses, or the great earthenware crock brimming with its snowy white liquid.

I don't know where Tutú found the energy to do everything she did while also caring for so many children, starting with us and followed by my nieces and nephews. She was never very long without at least one of us under her wing, and for all of us she was the most special person in the world, because she made us all feel special, too. Everything she did was extraordinary. In the morning, she lovingly peeled, grated, and strained a pineapple to make the most delicious pineapple juice in the world. And her corn dough for arepas, which she molded over and over, using her own closely-guarded techniques! One day I was helping her shell dry corn so she could soak the kernels in bleach for three days. We sat side by side, each working with her own corn cob, when she suddenly said in a quiet voice, perhaps speaking to herself, "And to think I could be living in Bogotá." My heart nearly stopped, because just the idea of living without Tutú by my side was inconceivable. But I breathed easier after she cleared her throat and took up the story of her godfather, an account that she'd started telling me several months earlier but then left hanging.

"My godfather was a very rich man, mi niña. He was one of the wealthy merchants of his day, early in the century. He had a mule team to transport merchandise between Bogotá and Barichara. This was very hard work, but it allowed him to take excellent care of his family, for example by putting his sons in the very best schools. One time when he was in Barichara, he told me 'Get ready Jesusa, because I'll take you with me on my next trip.' My father had just died, and it would have been a relief for my mother to have one less mouth to feed. She prepared a trunk of things I would take with me, the same trunk I have in my room today. While I waited for him to return, I opened my trunk every day to look at the things my mother had sacrificed so much to provide me with. I would take them out of the trunk to air them out in the sun, then put them away again before the day ended. But months went by and my godfather never returned. Finally, a man brought my mother the news. The mule train had been set upon by thieves, and when he put up resistance he was clubbed in the neck. His body was found because vultures were circling the place where it had been thrown off a cliff. The person who told us this said there was no sign of the lost merchandise or the mules. His whole family was suffering economically and had gone to work. Like so many others, my godfather spent part of his earnings on new merchandise and used the rest to support his family while waiting to be paid for what he sold. We never heard anything about his family again.

The day after we got this news, my mother told me to take my clothes out of the trunk and start using them, and the trunk could be used for storing other things. We never spoke about my trip again, especially after Mercedes disappeared."

"What do you mean? What happened to her?"

Tutú bit her tongue. She hadn't wanted to tell me this part of the story. It was still painful, but she knew that having heard this much, I'd eventually get the rest out of her with my endless questions.

"Mercedes had a boyfriend, and one festival day they absconded. Some friends of my father offered to hunt them down and bring them back, but they had a head start and they got away. We had no news of them for many months, until one April afternoon when I was gathering *hormigas culonas*, the large edible ants that are a local delicacy. My hands were all bitten up from the ants when I saw them coming over the ridge, and I yelled for my mother to come out of the house. When they got closer, I saw that Mercedes was carrying a bundle. It was her baby, my niece Carmen. It turned out that I had to care for her, the first baby I ever cared for, because I heard them arguing with my mother that night, and they left early the next morning. No matter what my mother said, they insisted that they'd get established in Bogotá within few months, and then they'd come back for her. But they never returned. My mother had to double her production of baked goods, barbecued meats, masato, and sweets, just to have a

97

few coins at the end of the week. That was barely enough for the three of us to survive on, and there was no money for my schooling, my shoes, or anything else. The little we could afford was for the baby, who had to have what any little girl her age would need. Of course, I helped my mother as much as I could, but I was a little girl, too. I did errands, delivered orders, and took care of the baby. I never played another children's game or climbed another tree, and there was no time for smiles. If I had any free time, it was only to play dolls with little Carmen. But Mamá often went out and left me to watch the pots on the stove, so Carmen would be alone in her crib, crying herself to sleep."

"I shed many a tear in those days, niña. When you're poor you have to learn to do whatever work you can get, and there's no time for games. You can't even imagine how much I missed the time I'd spent with José, playing in the countryside, free as birds. I missed my father deeply and silently hated my mother, especially at night. Sometimes I cried myself to sleep curled up in a corner where I could hear the owls outside. But I never sobbed, because I didn't want her to hear me. When I think back on this now, I ask my poor Mamá—may she rest in peace—to forgive me. She had a good heart and wanted only the best for me, and that was the only way she knew to get it. She was truly admirable, though. Not only was she poor, but she was a single woman in a macho world, with two girls to look out for. It's a pity she wasn't a man, because she had a good head for business. When the situation in Barichara got even more difficult, she packed her kitchen supplies in the trunk and announced that we were moving to Bucaramanga.

Leaving Barichara was painful. I knew nothing of the world other than that town, its people, and its plaza, and I couldn't begin to imagine what lay in the distance beyond the view from our ridgetop house. But my mother was a determined woman, and she'd announced her plans. I had nothing to say about it, and we were going to Bucaramanga.

We didn't get there all at once, though. When we got to Piedecuesta, the muleteer who was accompanying us got sick, and we couldn't go on without him. It was a hot day, and there wasn't even a hint of a breeze when my mother went off to find work and left me sitting in the plaza to watch our things. The wait seemed interminable in that heat, and by the time she returned, Carmen had fallen asleep and I was on the verge of doing the same. My mother shook my shoulder and made signs for me to follow her. Still drowsy, I lifted up the baby and saw the two boys who were following my mother and had taken charge of our things. As we walked along, Mamá informed me that "meanwhile" we'd be living with the Valenzuela family. She didn't say meanwhile what, but later I found out that she was trying to find other work for me, because the Valenzuelas had hired her as a cook, and just taking care of Carmen was all she could do. But I didn't even ask what would become of me. I'd received many blows in life, so what was one more? I'd been mentally and physically beside myself since we left Barichara. My mind was somewhere outside my body, and I could see everyone, even myself, from wherever that was. It was as though my body were not my own. Sometimes it walked on one side of me, and I could see it pass by, and other times my mind fell one, two, or three steps behind my body and I had to make an effort to keep up. My mind and body were reunited only at night, when I could feel the aches and pains of the day, especially my tired and battered feet, the cramping of my hands, and the weight of my arms. My body was young, but it was also old. I felt beaten down, empty, and apathetic. I didn't have the strength to cry, and I'd forgotten what it meant to pray. Now I know that my mother felt the same, because she'd long before forgotten how to smile, but at least she had control over her body, ordering it to get up in the morning and light the stove, to shell and grind corn, and to make hot chocolate while the arepas sizzled on the stovetop, all the while poking the fire to keep it hot. Morning after morning, every day the same. We knew it was Sunday only because we got up a little later and my mother had me put on my Sunday dress to go to mass with her while Carmen took a morning nap.

The church in Piedecuesta was ugly compared to 'my' church in Barichara, but once inside I remembered the prayers I'd forgotten so long before. While the priest celebrated the Latin mass, I prayed to my own sweet God to find me a job and relieve the unbearable burden on my mother. That's why I tell you that if we only pray to my dear, sweet God, he hears us. And now we're going to put on our pajamas, because it's time to go to sleep. Not another word, mi niña, your eyes are already half closed."

Tutú left me alone then, and I drifted off to sleep thinking about all she'd told me. Then I dreamt of mules lost in the wild, owls that swooped down for children on moonlit nights, fat culona ants frying in iron kettles, and my own loneliness, so much like the niña Tutú's own loneliness.

Tutú was an excellent reader. Unfortunately, she frequently got sidetracked, lost in her own thoughts or mixing what she was reading with stories from her own life. She seemed to have an unlimited number of anecdotes to draw on. But she didn't know how to write. My grandmother Lola taught her to read because she liked to be read to while embroidering. But Tutú sometimes skipped ahead in books, and if she didn't like the ending, she would change it. My grandmother never discovered this, probably because like me she was lulled to sleep by Tutú's reading, or simply because Tutú's endings were better than the originals.

But I'm getting ahead of myself. Tutú was about 14 years old when they got to Piedecuesta, and not long after that, somebody came to the Valenzuela's house to say that Dr. Daniel Peralta, a well-known doctor in Bucaramanga, needed a nanny because his wife was ill. My grandmother was physically and mentally weak, and she lost four babies for various reasons after having Inés. The last of these losses was particularly painful, since the child was born a 'blue baby.' He languished with this deadly condition for 15 days and then passed away in front of his helpless parents. While Daniel put this painful episode out of his mind by focusing on the needs of his patients, Lola shut herself in her room, closed the curtains, and let no one in, not even Inés. Least of all Inés. The best way to avoid attachments, she decided, was to avoid any personal ties, to have nothing to do with people, and to not even see anybody. After that, Inés could be seen wandering the hallways with a dog in her arms and several others following along behind her. They were her only company and her most faithful friends.

Daniel had little patience for children, but he was pained to see little sad-eyed Inés so alone and so serious at her five years of age. He decided to get her a nanny, and he chose Tutú on the recommendation of his good friend and patient Señor Valenzuela.

María de Jesús Rueda arrived at my grandfather's house with her trunk a few days later, and from that time on she was known as Tutú. Although she was not that much older than Inés, Tutú was more accustomed to heartache and loneliness. She quickly learned to discern Inés's moods, and if the girl was in a funk, she made no attempt to engage her. At other times, though, they got along spectacularly and played together as if they were the same age.

It wasn't long before Lola noticed the friendship between the two girls, and looked for ways to have Tutú spend part of the day with her. What she came up with was that she would teach Tutú to read, and this pretext worked like a charm. While Inés did her schoolwork, Lola taught Tutú to decipher first letters, then words, and finally the way words are woven into phrases. These lessons were sufficient for both of them, and neither saw any need for Tutú to learn to write. What for? She didn't need writing to fulfill any of her many responsibilities, and any time taken to learn such a difficult skill would only distract her from her prescribed tasks. Soon she began to spend time with Lola in the afternoon while Inés napped. This was before Lola, who had recovered from her crisis, prepared to go out visiting, or if it was Thursday to receive visitors.

Those Thursdays with their afternoon visits were very busy. Mornings were spent preparing refreshments, and before long Tutú was known for her delicious preparations. The economic situation was improving in Bucaramanga, and there were many invitations to banquets, soirées, and picnics. All the hosts sought to outdo each other, and Delfina was hired to oversee the food preparation for one of these parties. She was very successful, and after that she was much in demand for such events. This was very positive for Tutú, because even though Piedecuesta was close by, it wasn't easy for her to see her mother without a good excuse.

Delfina was now in demand in Bucaramanga, and they were frequently seen together. Sometimes, Tutú even got permission to leave the house and go help her. Inés didn't cause many problems. Once she learned to read, she lost herself in the world of books. Sometimes she spent whole afternoons in her armchair, always in the company of her dogs, whom she preferred to any toy or human being. Only in books did she reconnect with her own inner life or experience emotions that she did not otherwise confront. She laughed and cried along with the characters, sharing their dreams and enjoying the affection of nurturing mothers, the smiles of affectionate fathers, and the intimate and sometimes mischievous companionship of the siblings she never had. Her life outside books was limited to daily hygiene, doing homework, going on rare outings with girls of her age, and sporadic visits with her cousins, whose boisterous joie de vivre helped her forget her own dull and monotonous existence.

Tutú understood this very well because she felt the same way now, but unlike Inés, she had once known the pleasure of playing freely, running in the fields, climbing trees, breaking new trails to places unknown, chasing butterflies, and trapping edible ants, a long list of enjoyable activities and memorable experiences denied to this poor little rich girl that she cared for. Sometimes she felt sorry for her. How ironic. Tutú was a poor orphan, resigned to servitude, who felt sorry for a girl who slept under silk sheets, whose every need was satisfied, and who had no obligations other than to stay alive, grow up healthy, and eventually marry and have children.

But you can't judge your life based on what you have, Tutú told me while recounting these things. Life is a succession of memories woven tightly together until they form strong and durable moorings that tether you to the earth. That's what Inés lacked, and her only substitute for it was an absorption in books. In books she lived vicariously through the colorful lives of others, so different from her own solitary, colorless, and grim existence.

"Tell me what you're doing, Tutú…"

My voice seemed to surprise her, and she almost dropped the jar that was balanced on her lap.

"These kids… Why do they have to appear out of nowhere when you don't even know where they came from? One of these days I'm gonna have some kind of attack if you're determined to startle me."

"Oh, Tutú, don't say that. I didn't mean to scare you. Admit it, you were in your own world and you didn't hear me coming."

"That's true, mi niña. Forgive me. I was reminiscing. When you get old, all you've got are memories. And I'm very, very rich in memories, niña."

"So, are you gonna tell me what you're doing?"

"Well, do you remember when I told you what day it is tomorrow?"

I interrupted her impatiently:

"Of course, I remember. It's May 3rd, the day of the Holy Cross."

"That's right. And I also told you that on the day of the Holy Cross I have to say Jesus's name 1,000 times so the devil doesn't take me off when I die."

"Look, Tutú. First of all, let's just say you're not gonna die, okay? Second, I don't believe in the devil, but with all the praying you do, he wouldn't dare take you off, anyway."

Tutú stifled a laugh and reached out to twist a lock of my constantly tangled hair between her fingers, then patted the stool by her side.

"Sit here and help me count the 100 kernels of corn that I need. Tomorrow I'll move them from one jar to another ten times while repeating *When I die the devil will be powerless against me because on the day of the Holy Cross I said 'Jesus' one thousand times."*

"And when we finish counting the kernels," she said, "let's make the May cross."

And that's what we did. We counted the 100 kernels, then went to the garden and snipped all kinds of flowers. Several days before, she'd had her *comadre* María make a large cross of mountain laurel, and now we decorated it with all the flowers we'd collected. When it was ready, we tied it up on the tallest tree in the garden. It was really a work of art. I was very proud that she'd chosen me to help her with the cross that year, but that was far from the last time. From that day, on we repeated the ritual every May. First we counted the kernels of corn, then we made the cross and hung it up, and finally, satisfied, we sat down together to admire our artwork.

Tutú spent the next day sitting on her stool and patiently moving the 100 kernels of corn from one jar to another, moving her lips as she repeatedly and inaudibly spoke the name "Jesus." Having watched her year after year, I easily recognized the syllables of "Jesus" on her lips, which she repeated 1,000 times as each kernel clinked against the bottom of the jar.

I found her praying in the kitchen on many other occasions, and I was not surprised when she told me that she was praying for this or that neighbor who had come by to pay their last respects and say adiós. Everyone in the house knew that Tutú saw beings that were not visible to us. Same with Mamá. One day when Tutú and I had a long talk, she told me that on a couple of occasions she'd actually seen the woman that my mother saw come into the room.

Although she never learned who the woman was, she had a feeling that something important had happened there. During my childhood, my mother continued to have nightmares in which she followed the woman and heard her say "It was here," but she never said what "it" was.

Both Tutú and Mamá had access to dimensions that were off limits to most of us. Maybe that's why there was a special connection between them.

ॐ

One day, Mamá told me that Tutú was very sick. I immediately felt a drowning sensation and a pain in my heart. I couldn't bring myself to ask for details, but I wouldn't have been able to anyway, because my throat was closing up tight. For many years, I'd imagined the moment when someone would tell me that Tutú would no longer be by my side, and now my deepest fear was coming true, but it was far worse than I'd ever imagined.

I ran from the room. Perhaps if I distanced myself quickly from my mother's painful words, I could make them go away. I could buy a little more time, be a little more prepared for what was to come. But this was not to be. Carmen had come days before and taken Tutú away——with her trunk, of course. From my room, I heard her swear to Mamá that she'd care for her to the end, and I'm sure that my mother was as dubious as I was, but like me, she felt powerless to change anything. She and Tutú had shared a life, but she had no legal say in her fate.

I didn't say goodbye when they left, and I didn't cry. All I did was open my underwear drawer and inhale the scent of rosemary that drifted out. It had been some time since Tutú had been able to add fresh sprigs of rosemary every week, but I'd been doing it for her. Until that day, that is. After that I never went back to her rosemary bush.

Years later, I planted a rosemary cutting in her memory, and I watched it evolve into a healthy bush. Although I didn't pick sprigs of rosemary to put in my underwear drawer, I smiled every time I went to the garden and saw it flowering, because I always thought to myself that Tutú was somewhere hanging out diapers on a rosemary bush.

From the day Tutú left the house, I understood inside that I'd never see her again. I didn't say anything when my mother gave me the news that she was very sick, but I understood the inevitable.

I went to school that afternoon as always. I wrote my name and the date May 3 on a social studies exam, but then I lay down my pencil and angrily wiped a tear from my cheek, while my lips moved and I silently repeated Jesus, Jesus, Jesus…

❧

Tutú took care of me, but she also ministered in a very special way to my yearnings, my fragile self-esteem, and my deep sadness. I never heard her bemoan her fate, speak ill of another, or complain about the hard work she'd performed from an early age. She always had a smile on her face, a kind word on her lips, and words of praise. She was the only person in my childhood who called me pretty; she was the person who best understood my moods, and she was the only one who recognized my rebelliousness as a cry for help in a world indifferent to my pain.

Tutú personifies my conception of unconditional love, which she always gave me. It's a kind of love that I've otherwise gotten only from my dogs, especially Mateo, who left me 18 years ago but whose memory I hold dear to this day, so compellingly that his absence still hurts. Someday I'd like to write the story of Mateo, perhaps to open with words like those used by Juan Ramón Jiménez to begin his book: *"Platero is small and hairy…so soft to the touch that he might be said to be made of cotton,"* because my little Mateo was like that.

I'm sure that Mateo is sleeping now at Tutú's feet as she prays the rosary. When he awakens, he looks at her adoringly and she strokes his head. I know this because every time it happens, the world smiles upon me and I have a good day.

https://www.youtube.com/watch?v=8RZeHO7gBJk

Toitico bien empacao (Katie James)

The Pain of Loss

Bernardo was more than two years older than me, but we were inseparable, joined at the hip. Until we grew into adolescence, that is, and our hormones stirred us up in different ways.

I don't think we misbehaved any more or less than many other children our age, but we always managed to get ourselves into trouble. It was I who was punished, of course, either because he was faster to run and hide in the shed behind the house, or simply because I was the perfect target for our mother's anger and her arm of steel. By the time she was done with me, she was satisfied and left him in peace.

In any case, not even our fear of Mamá kept us from sneaking into the spare room while she took her afternoon siesta. This room still contained the flasks used by my grandfather Dr. Peralta to mix his preparations. My grandfather was a pharmacist as well as a physician, and he left an extensive pharmacopeia—which we still have—describing all his remedies.

Many of the mysterious liquids had evaporated, and many of the flasks no longer had labels, but we always found something to experiment with. One day we opened a bottle marked "ether," and we waited to see if it would work, if we would lose consciousness, that is. But nothing happened. I don't think it was really the fault of the ether, though. That room was very hot, and after a while we ran to the kitchen for lemonade. We were dedicated researchers, though, so the next day we tried chloroform with the same negative result. Our research was not progressing due to constant lemonade breaks, so we decided to experiment with an animal subject.

Lacking any better ideas, we set our eyes on Toby, Adriana's rabbit. Adriana had gotten Toby in a *piñata*, and I swear he must have found the cake from Alice in Wonderland, because he grew to enormous proportions. Once we realized what was happening, he was about 20 inches long, he hopped up stairs two at a time, and he got into any room by kicking the door open. Most recently, he'd been waging a campaign against Bernardo, soiling his bed more than once with urine so foul-smelling that it could knock you over before you even walked in the door.

The first thing we did was build a cage strong enough to contain the monster. Then we selected the most horrible-smelling leaves we could find in the garden and ground them into a paste, which we gave Toby to inhale. Total success on our second attempt! He fell to the floor of the cage and slept so soundly for two uninterrupted hours that Adriana thought we'd killed him. Thus ended our experimentation with live subjects.

Our next area of interest was entomology. At that time, there was an infestation of cicadas in Bucaramanga, and since Bernardo knew everything or set out to learn whatever he didn't yet know, we spent a couple of weeks researching how long they could stay alive underground. We were unable to complete this experiment because the gardener complained that the garden was full of holes, and that morning he'd broken one of our jars with a shovel when he tried to see what kind of pests were producing the holes. By the time we heard Mamá's war cry, we'd already taken off for the roof and our customary period of exile.

It seemed that we were running out of scientific fields, but the problem was that our experiments were being cut short due to factors beyond our control. We thought we might have more success with chemistry, so we turned to that field with all the energy and determination of a six-year-old and an eight-year-old. We knew that Roberto had gunpowder in his room because he'd been conducting experiments at school. We secretly borrowed enough of his powder to conduct a couple of experiments without him knowing that we'd dipped into his valued supply.

The bad part was that we didn't account for the spy in our midst. We'd loaded a rocket with powder, but after it exploded, a certain individual conveyed this valuable intelligence to Mamá. When we learned of this development, we hurriedly abandoned the launch site and made tracks for the sanctuary of the roof. Perhaps as a result, we lost our enthusiasm for rocketry.

We launched our first profitable business on that roof. The gardener had planted a loofah vine that climbed the wall and grew exuberantly there. I don't remember who taught us to peel and wash the loofahs, but I suppose it was the gardener. In any case, either the pedagogy was outstanding or the students were first rate. Either way, we spent about a week in voluntary exile and produced ready-to-use loofahs that Bernardo then sold to Mamá and the household staff. We earned enough to divide the proceeds and begin to pay for an electric train. Unfortunately, we didn't consider the law of supply and demand. The gardener hadn't advised us of this factor, regarding which he may also have been unaware.

One day, we discovered that nobody at the house was interested in buying loofahs anymore, because we'd saturated the market. The loofah vine stopped producing shortly thereafter, which was just as well.

⟋

My parents frequently travelled to Venezuela because food was very cheap there, and because they could get canned goods that were unavailable in Colombia. We all enjoyed the five-hour road trip, during which we drove through multiple climate zones. From the moderate temperatures of Bucaramanga, we ascended to the bone-chilling páramo of Santurbán and then reached Pamplona, a cold city with an ever-present cloud cover. Then we descended to hot and dusty Cúcuta. It was an easy drive from there to our destination, and despite the heat we had a glorious two days buying whatever trifles caught our eye, while Mamá filled the trunk with non-perishable goods to replenish the pantry.

As soon as we had money to buy the model train we'd seen in a store window the previous year, we took advantage of the next Venezuela trip and hurried to the store to buy it. We opened the box at least a thousand times in the hotel that night, minutely inspecting every aspect of the train. Naturally, the ride back home was long and boring, because we couldn't wait to get there and assemble our beautiful train set.

The train track was very small, a circle of just about 20 inches in diameter, so we immediately began saving to enlarge it. On our next trip, we bought more sections of track and one or two more cars. Our poor locomotive struggled to pull the longer train, and Bernardo declared that the transformer was overheating. We had no choice but to buy another transformer, but then we realized that with two transformers we needed another locomotive. This process kept us very busy, but it seemed there was no end in sight. Papá was pleased that we were spending less time up in the trees, because this meant fewer damaged branches, and the gardener was grateful that we weren't making his work more difficult and he could keep the grounds impeccable. And in retrospect, Mamá didn't scold us as much unless our arguments over the control of the transformer were so loud that they bothered her in her room.

But we didn't play with the trains all the time. We spent a good part of the day climbing trees, reading comic books and adventure stories, and planning new escapades.

We'd recently discovered the joys of cinema, and since we were no longer investing our meager savings in train tracks, we used them for movie tickets whenever possible. Sometimes we went alone, and sometimes with friends, but Bernardo always chose the movies we went to. He had the last word in everything, in fact, even when to cross the street. Then he'd stride across the road purposefully, while I ran to keep up.

In the evening after the movies, we'd camp out in Bernardo's room to discuss what we'd seen. I was continually amazed at how wise and intelligent he was. I always wondered when I would be so wise. I must confess that this hasn't happened yet, or if it has, I never realized it. Bernardo knew everything about everything, and everything that he made with his own hands was perfect. He liked to build boats and planes, he drew flawlessly with India ink, and since he had an excellent ear for music, he was selected to be the drum major of the school band. Like everyone else in the family, he had an inherent tendency to lose his temper if provoked, but most of the time this could be avoided if you changed the subject.

One day I discovered that he was growing taller and taller (he eventually reached a height of almost 6"1'), while I was filling out in the places where girls do. We no longer had the same interests. Sometimes we listened to music and argued because I liked the Bee Gees and he preferred the Ángeles Negros. He was more prone to anger and he had less patience for my foolishness. We continued to be good friends, though, even though he spent less time at home after discovering a passion for hunting and fishing. In the end, this drove us apart because I've never been comfortable with either of those activities. I just don't like the idea of killing, especially when it comes to defenseless animals.

I spent hours reading while he was out of the house, partly just to isolate myself and avoid problems as much as possible. Once in a while, we would run into each other in the kitchen and chat over a cup of coffee as we had before, but we had increasingly less to talk about. We both wanted to study medicine, so when he went to Bogotá to follow that dream, everyone thought it was the most normal thing in the world. I was still in high school, and at the last minute I thought better of a career in medicine for several important reasons: I panicked at the sight of blood (I still do), my hand trembled when I picked up a scalpel, and I had never been good at staying up late. And as you might expect, I was smitten with the first boy to show interest in me. But that's another story.

Getting back to Bernardo, though. He graduated, got married, and came back to Bucaramanga. He was still in his early days practicing medicine when he met his untimely end. It was a horrible accident and a sordid scandal that shocked the city, and rumors and gossip were repeated endlessly in certain circles. I won't go into these things because they're beside the point.

The event that ended Bernardo's life was so sudden and unexpected that it caught me unprepared. The death of a loved one is very difficult, and we are not taught to move through our grief before we are actually faced with a loss. And while this was the death of a young man with a promising future, it meant much more to me on a personal level. For more than a month, I didn't have the energy for anything but bathing and sitting in my armchair embroidering. My tears did not come, but I put stitch after stitch on a piece of cloth, mixed with occasional drops of blood when I stuck my finger. By the end of the month, I finished the embroidery and my period of mourning, but I'll never fill the emptiness in my heart left by the loss of my playmate.

Something was missing from my life, and it took me many years to discover what it was. That's why this chapter has no conclusion. In closing, I will just repeat Bernardo's name and thank him for having shared a difficult childhood with me. Without your help, brother, my days would have been less enjoyable, and my nights would have been longer, more bedeviled by nightmares.

https://www.youtube.com/watch?v=jUWBXnTxxMI

Murió la flor (Los Ángeles Negros)

Detachment

It's said that the devil gives nieces and nephews to those whom God does not give children. I don't believe in the malevolent figure concocted by the Catholic Church to frighten us, but I truly believe that the existence of Cata, Roberto's daughter, was one of the signs that God provided to help me decipher my mission in life.

Sometimes special people are lent us for a short time, as though we are being told to make the most of the few minutes we are destined to share with them.

Cata and I got along extraordinarily well from the time she was very young. In fact, she touched my soul from the first day I lay eyes on her. She was like an alter ego to me, absolutely the daughter I never had. We yakked it up, painted together, laughed like crazy, and shared everything from our love of animals to our delight in wildflowers and roasting

129

marshmallows. She came into my life at just the right time, and I learned enough from my time with her to fill a library.

Cata was a very special person, but she left this life just when I needed her most. She closed her eyes for the last time on a January afternoon after three months of cancer. Her last words were "I want to go home."

Many years passed before I understood the meaning of those words. I'd studied in a Catholic school and learned all about the resurrection, but in this as in many other teachings, there was something that didn't seem quite right to me about it.

I joined a healing group shortly after Cata left us, and I spent fifteen years processing the pain of her senseless loss. I alleviated my suffering and I brought comfort to others. I studied techniques such as Spiritual Healing, Pranic Healing, Reiki, and Reconnective Healing.® Based on what I learned, I came to understand that we pass through this life on our way home to reunite with our essential nature.

Though she was only ten years old, Cata already understood this.

In Cata's last week on earth, I began to read her The Little Prince, but we didn't get past the chapter where the little prince allows the snake to bite him so he can return to his flower. That night, I understood that Cata's body was no longer useful to her and she wanted to return to the home from which she had come to enrich our lives, albeit for ten short years.

Who knows how many flowers Cata has in her garden? I can see her frolicking among them with her little lamb, whom she will have taught not to eat the roses.

When you lose a loved one, the pain of their loss is only slightly allayed by your memories of them, and by your choice to smile because you had them while they were here, rather than cry because they are gone.

The day came when I lost my beautiful dog Mateo as well, and a couple of years later my husband and I separated. I was devastated by so many losses, and by the time I heard about the Camino de Santiago, it seemed that I was hitting rock bottom. I looked further into the pilgrimage, and in desperation, I set out with my backpack, planning to walk an ambitious 12.5 miles per day.

I learned that three kinds of people hike the Camino: those who are seeking a religious reawakening, those who walk for the exercise, and those who are looking for an inexpensive tourist experience. People in the latter group often follow the trail for a week or two at most, while the entire Camino takes at least 33 days if you walk 9-12 miles per day. When I decided to go for it, I thought that a one-week trip wouldn't do justice to my three months of preparation, so I'd walk for 18 days. I wasn't sure what my goal was, so I'd just put one foot in front of the other. I was in for a big surprise.

I arrived in Saint-Jean-Pied-de-Port with my backpack weighing about 22 pounds. I had a walking stick, a pair of good walking shoes, and a brimmed hat for the sun. With so much preparation under my belt, I believed that I was ready to meet the challenge. But nothing prepared me for the first day.

I left the hostel at daybreak with a young German woman. It was still quite dark, and we were the only people in the otherwise deserted streets. My glasses were in the backpack, so I gave my companion the map. That was my first mistake.

Our goal for the day was reach Roncesvalles, on the other side of the Pyrenees. It was a mostly uphill path with spectacular views. After half an hour we came to a wayside inn, where the French owner began to give us directions. I speak no French, so I went to the rest room while my companion talked to him. That was my second mistake, and probably my first important lesson. To others, I seemed bold, sure of myself, and rebellious. But I'd always depended on others for my happiness. I thought they'd tell me what to do, where to go, and how to get there.

As soon as we left the hostel it started to rain, and then it began to come down in torrents. In just a few minutes my shoes were soaked, and my feet started sloshing around inside them. I announced to my companion that I needed to pour out the rainwater and wring out my socks. She said that if she stopped walking, she would die of cold, so she kept on going. It took me a while to put myself back together, because as soon as I wrang the water out of each sock, the other was soaked again. I repeated this process two or three times, and when I was finally ready, I set out to catch up to my companion. Unfortunately, I never saw her again.

My first two errors were self-evident when I came to a fork in the trail. I had no map, and no idea whether to go left or right. The road descended to the left, but the yellow arrow of the Camino seemed to point right. I hesitated for a few seconds and then set out to the right, only to discover that the trail disappeared, and I was enveloped in a thick fog. I attempted to backtrack, but I was completely disoriented. It was still raining and it was getting bitter cold. Frustrated, I decided to advance in the same direction as before. At least the fog seemed less uniformly dense in that direction.

I must have walked for at least an hour and a half in that cold rain. I headed downhill on some goat paths, but when they petered out, I looked desperately for any sign that I was (or was not) headed in the right direction. "Have trust," a voice told me, "the French-Spanish border can't be completely desolate in the twenty-first century." This voice told me not to lose faith, and I decided that sooner or later I'd come upon a native of these mountains who would help me. Nothing of the sort! But I suddenly spied an indistinct blue shape downhill and to the right.

I headed in that direction, and when I got closer, I saw that it was a figure in a blue poncho, bent over like a person looking at their feet. I called out to this person but got no response. I didn't know what to do, but I looked around and suddenly saw a trail marker. It was the yellow arrow of the Camino and it pointed downhill, the same way I'd been headed. I continued downward, faster now, but when I got to where I'd seen the figure, there was nothing there. It was as though they'd been swallowed by the thick fog, poncho and all.

Now I understand that someone had come to my aid. The words "have trust" stand out in my mind, because I remembered the voice telling me that, and I felt that I was accompanied.

Those who know say that the Camino de Santiago gives you no more or less than what you are looking for. I didn't even know it, but I had many questions, and little by little they were being answered. One day I was thinking about Cata when her favorite song by José Luis Perales began to play on my ipod. It was the song that her friends had sung at her funeral. My knees hurt so much and my backpack was so heavy that I understood then and there that I hadn't let go of her, just as I hadn't let

136

go of Bernardo or of my dog Mateo. I still carried the heavy weight of their loss on my shoulders. And in what was at least a symbolic recognition of this fact, I made a package when I got to the first town, sending my ipod and various other heavy and unnecessary items back to Italy, where the rest of my luggage was.

https://www.youtube.com/watch?v=_4ntU0T4v0s

Que canten los niños (José Luis Perales)

∾

On that same night, a conversation with another person on the path turned out to be a cathartic experience. Each of us had an urgent need to let go of what was weighing us down, and to free the loved ones we continued to mourn without fully releasing them. We'd both read a lot and understood the need for detachment, but we weren't applying what we knew to our lives. On that starry night in the north of Spain, we consoled each other and agreed to work on this problem. Then we sealed our pact with a fraternal hug and went off to sleep. When I got up the next morning he was gone, and I never saw him again. But I didn't need him anymore.

The Camino de Santiago is like that: difficult, intense, and demanding, but also liberating. The 12 days I was physically alone were spent in constant meditation. As a spiritual retreat, it was a time for healing and an opportunity to free my soul of the ghosts that afflicted it. I was constantly reminded that I was not really alone. A being more powerful than myself was always walking by my side and leading me by the hand. One day, for example, I'd used up my water. As soon as I started thinking about this, I came to a spring. On another day, I was tired of staying at hostels and wanted to spend the night at a hotel. Like magic, a hotel appeared as I entered a town. I found rosemary bushes in the most unexpected places and stopped to sample their familiar aroma. Tutú was there with me, I told myself.

And the Camino gives us what we need. One day I noticed that I was thinking more about the blisters on my feet than about the divine signs I'd been receiving, which were becoming less frequent. I was sure that when I got home, I'd be strengthened by all the lessons learned on those arduous 18 days of walking in the rain or under an oppressive sun, often hungry and bone tired, and spending my nights trying to sleep amidst snoring hikers.

In retrospect, I believe I could have saved myself from all this, but it was what I needed at the time. My experience on the trail helped me draw on many object lessons accumulated over the years, and with them construct a coherent understanding of myself as a person. My life had become a puzzle whose scattered pieces I was able to reassemble, allowing me to begin a new, freer, stage in which I accept responsibility for my role on earth.

I came to love myself in my time on the Camino, and to take ownership of my decisions, my actions, and my future. By the time I got home, I was sure of my continued progress. My doubts, fears, and distress were left behind in the red dust of the Castilian Plateau, in the sleepy towns I'd passed through, in the sweat of my brow on the final days of my arduous pilgrimage, and in the eyes of other seekers like myself. I'd found the key to the mystery of life.

Disappointments

As I mentioned above, Cupid shot an arrow straight through my heart when I was barely 19 years old.

When I got married, I thought that I'd found the key to happiness. I believed that I knew how to navigate the twists and turns on the road of life, and that I didn't need anyone else's help. I believed that after my unhappy childhood, I had a right to happiness and that I'd achieve it in my marriage. Oh, really? It didn't matter that I had to give up a couple of things, that I had to abjectly submit to my husband's wishes on more than one occasion, or that I had to postpone my plans because it wasn't the right time to pursue them.

After getting married, I got a bachelor's degree in bacteriology. I wanted to work, but my husband's travel plans always got in the way, and I never found a job that would allow me to combine work, marriage, and travel. I'd taken two years of German, and then I also studied English and Italian. I soon became a medical translator, and I now have 30 years of experience in that field. It's been professionally satisfying, and it has led to many friendships around the world.

From the beginning of my marriage, I discovered that two things were lacking: love and laughter. This didn't seem important when I was 19 years old, and I thought that I had enough love for both of us. Sure, with all the love in my heart there must have been plenty to go around, right? Well, no. My father used to say "nothing can work if it's all give and no take," and it didn't. We lived together, ate together, and travelled together, but that was it. At the most, we were companions, but that wasn't enough for me, and I began to change. I laughed less. I was increasingly less interested in pleasing him, and I felt more and more alone in our big house. Finally I put it into words: I wasn't happy.

My four-legged friend Mateo had faithfully provided me with love, strength, and companionship for 14 years, and then one day he died. My world was coming to pieces, and I felt lost, trapped, and empty.

One day my husband had the courage to say what was maybe the hardest thing in his life: "I don't love you and I've never loved you." What can you say if your husband tells you such a thing? I'd always been proud to tell the absolute truth, even if it was painful, but now I faced the heartbreaking reality that my 33 and a half years of marriage had been a colossal lie, a sham, and a deception.

That's when my world was stood on its head, and the forces that had characterized my life came crashing into view: callous indifference, lack of forgiveness, mourning, loss, and disconnection. It took me two years to learn about myself and to unlearn the unfortunate parts of myself that had led me to this point, and it took my experience on the Camino de Santiago to give me the internal fortitude I needed to reinvent my life. I was ready to love again.

There was one minor detail I hadn't taken into consideration. When you're fifty-something, men your age are looking for women thirty years old (or less). But that doesn't matter, I told myself, it's just a matter of looking for the right man. There's a soulmate out there for everyone.

So I set out on a search that took me far and wide, and I came across males of every conceivable description. I won't bore you with all the details, apart from the three who lasted more than one month each.

☙

The man I'll call Narcissus was as self-satisfied as his namesake in Greek mythology. He was the best looking and most successful man he knew. His mother had been beautiful, his daughter was uncommonly attractive, and his sister was gorgeous. To top it off, he'd married the most glamorous woman in the world. There was not a woman who didn't fall at his feet.

It's true that he had many good qualities. He was good-natured and even-tempered, and he was not looking to be tied down. This was perfect for me, because at that moment, I wasn't looking for a committed relationship either. I simply wasn't ready.

The problem was that he recalled aloud how all the women in his life had been gorgeous, flawless, and one of a kind, and I understood that I was not on his list of remarkables. It had been a long time since anyone had said such lovely things to me— things that all women want to hear—and I concluded that there was no need to wait any longer, so I left him to enjoy his memories of breathtaking beauty.

Then Mercury appeared, fresh from foreign shores. He had a boatload of stories and a well-honed ability to convince others of his exceptional qualities. After knowing him for a month, I understood his game plan. All his savings were tied up in his fabulous car, and his pension was barely enough to pay his rent. His proposal was that we join forces. Simply put, that I would adopt him and take responsibility for his needs. Then I fell ill with a virus, and he demonstrated his disinterest and lack of concern for my well-being. I understood that he did not represent a solution, either.

A few months later, I met Peter Pan. He was intelligent, he told endless anecdotes, and he knew how to make me laugh. I almost surrendered to his charms, but lucky for me, he quickly showed his cards. He talked incessantly about men who had a Peter Pan syndrome, until I discovered that he was one of them. He was unable to make commitments, preferring to keep his options open and to have several balls in the air at the same time. What a shame.

It's not hard to imagine that after these experiences I was ready to take a vow of lifelong chastity. I was fed up with men, with game playing, and with self-centered hucksters. I decided to focus on my translation work while continuing to pursue the not-for-profit healing that I've always practiced.

146

One day a book called Reconnective Healing® fell into my hands, and I found that the authors were sponsoring a course the following month. To say that this changed my life would be an understatement. From the moment I finished the course, things fell into place and everything began to go well for me. Life began to smile on me, and it was with new enthusiasm that I prepared for a trip with a layover in Puerto Rico. Little did I know that destiny had a surprise waiting for me there.

https://www.youtube.com/watch?v=bCXabYdHSpY

Mucho corazón (Ema Elena Valdelamar)

Love Comes Knocking

My flight to Puerto Rico was very enjoyable. As it turned out, my seatmate was a Protestant minister who started flirting with me within the first half hour. Nonetheless, I was firm in my commitment to eliminate the word "men" from my vocabulary and hold to the vow of chastity I'd made just six months before when I dispatched Peter Pan back to Never-Never Land. Though the minister and I merely chatted amicably for the rest of the flight, my traveling companions took the opportunity to jokingly anoint me the *femme fatale* of the group.

The next day I was going to meet my friend Gloria and her husband at 9 a.m., and I was punctual as always. I got on the elevator, and just before the doors closed, a short man with glasses stepped on. I didn't know him, but my mother had taught me to be courteous (or else), so I automatically bid him good morning. While the elevator descended from the sixth floor to the first, the man, who was from the United States, asked me if I was Puerto Rican.

"No, I said, I'm, Colombian. And you?"

"I'm from Ohio, he said, but I'm here for work." Then the doors opened, and he walked out to the left. He was going to Starbucks, I imagined, and I turned toward the restaurant on the right. Since my friends had joked so recently about my instant attractions, the first thing I said to them was:

"I just picked up a guy in the elevator."

But after a minimal back-and-forth on the subject, we forgot about it. The delicious aroma of the morning coffee distracted us, and we began to talk about more practical things, such as planning our tourist activities on the Island of Enchantment.

At around noon, Gloria practically dragged me into a church. As soon as we crossed the threshold we saw a glass case, one of those Catholic churches use to sell prayer cards, rosary beads, saint stickers, and scapulars. And as it happened, the most prominent *novena*, (a booklet with prayers that are said for nine days) was of Saint Anthony, known to seek out eligible men for single women and who knows what else. For some reason, many desperate women even set out a figurine of Saint Anthony standing on his head, but to tell you the truth, that seems a little odd to me.

"Buy that novena and I'll pray it with you," Gloria said. So I bought it, perhaps more to indulge her than out of any real wish to pray for nine days.

I got up very early the next morning to take a walk on the beach and see the sunrise. As I checked to make sure I had my room key, I spied the same man who was on the elevator the previous day. This time he was coming out of a room across the hall. He must have seen me too, because when I got to the elevator, he was holding the doors open for me.

"I'm going to the treadmill on the 10th floor, he said almost apologetically." These gringos are really strange, I thought. Who'd want to go to a smelly, air conditioned gym when they could go outside to a beautiful sandy beach under a brilliant blue sky?

"I'm going for a walk on the beach," I said, hoping he would feel a twinge of envy.

As on the day before, I met Gloria and her husband for breakfast at nine. We made plans for the day and left the hotel for Old San Juan. As soon as we started to walk, we came to another church. This was no surprise, since the city was founded by Spanish Catholics. Nor was it surprising when Gloria immediately invited me to go in with them.

"Oh, no, thanks. After yesterday, I think I've filled my quota of churches for the rest of the year. You guys go and I'll wait for you in the park."

I chose a bench in the shade and took out my brand new camera to study all the functions I wasn't familiar with. I got so absorbed in this that when I looked up, more than 20 minutes had passed. I was alone in the park and there was no sign of my friends. So I went to the church and found that a mass was underway. "They must have gotten involved in the mass and stayed," I thought. But I didn't see them, so I proceeded quickly to our next stop, which was a pharmacy. They weren't there

153

either, so I went back to the park and entered the church by a different door. Finally, I realized that like Robinson Crusoe, I was alone on an island. I had no phone, which wouldn't have helped anyway since I didn't know their number. "I must have crossed paths with them when I went to the pharmacy," I said to myself. "Maybe I'll find them on our agreed route." So I started walking more briskly, because I thought they must have gotten a head start. After a few blocks, I came to a tourist office, and it seemed like a good idea to ask how to get to the restaurant that Gloria had chosen because she'd read that it served the best piña colada on the island. I casually asked the young woman behind the counter for directions to a restaurant called Aromas on Tetuán Street. It took her a few minutes, which seemed very odd to me if it was such a famous restaurant, but she eventually wrote an address on a small piece of paper and explained how to get there. It wasn't far, but when I got to the address on Tetuán Street, it was only a small cafeteria with an inconspicuous sign that said Aromas.

I should have realized that something was wrong when I ordered a beer and the waiter told me that they didn't serve alcohol. How could this be the place with the best piña colada on the island? But I was tired of walking, and I took a seat to wait for them. Half an hour later, they still hadn't arrived, so I ordered something to eat. It was just about then that the downpour began. There was still no sign of them when I finished eating, but it had stopped raining. Reinvigorated by my meal, I got on one of the free buses that drive tourists around the city. I looked for my friends, but after two or three circuits, I'd seen all the passengers and they never made an appearance. Then I decided to give up looking and take a cab back to the hotel. I told myself that they were adults and they could take care of themselves very well without me.

At the reception desk they told me that Gloria had left me a message:

"You got lost, *amiga*. Come along, we're waiting for you at the mall."

155

Unfortunately, the mall is huge, and I was tired of aimlessly looking for them. I deleted the message and was just opening the drawer to get out my bathing suit when the phone rang.

A male voice was on the other end, and he spoke to me in English.

"Are you Colombian?"

Since it wasn't Gloria and I didn't know anyone else there, I was sure that the call had to be from the reception desk. "Am I Colombian?" I thought to myself. "Of course, I'm Colombian, but why is he asking?" That's when my heart started racing and my blood started to pound through my veins. I imagined myself in a movie where an unknown man called to say that something terrible had happened to my friends. But why was this man speaking to me in English?

At first, I understood only a few fragments like "elevator," and "are you married," but then I clearly heard the phrase "go out to eat."

Yes, the voice on the telephone belonged to the gringo I'd met in the elevator and with whom I'd exchanged some minimal pleasantries. Now I imagined a different movie, where my body would be found chopped to pieces in the trunk of a broken-down car abandoned in a back alley. And in Puerto Rico, no less, with all the difficulties of repatriating cadavers. I tried to think of a polite way to turn down the invitation, so I told him that my friends were AWOL.

"How about a drink in the bar while you wait for them?"

Well, that would be different, because I could leave a message at the reception desk to tell them where I was, and nothing would happen to me unless the gringo drugged me and dragged me out of the hotel. So I accepted. I put my bathing suit back in the drawer, took a shower, and went down to the bar to meet him. I was sure that he'd told me his name, but with all my anxiety I hadn't remembered it. To be honest, I didn't even remember what he looked like. And I certainly didn't imagine that I was on my way to a date with destiny.

As he'd said, he was in the bar waiting for me. Another alarm went off: "Oh, shoot. Who knows how long he's been here drinking?" And I planned a quick escape: "Just one beer. I'll get a beer and if he's a pain in the neck I'll go to the bathroom and disappear."

Meanwhile, Bill (how embarrassing, I had to ask his name) was sitting in front of a tall rum and coke. Later he told me that he preferred beer but he wanted to seem sophisticated. So there we were, playing a sort of cat and mouse. Each of us had the wrong drink for some mixed-up reason, since I would have preferred a glass of wine.

After an hour, I realized that neither of us had finished our drink, but we hadn't stopped talking for a moment.

He told me that he was an architect and was in Puerto Rico for work, but he'd decided to stay till Sunday and get in another couple of beach days.

Much later, he told me that he'd been planning to change his ticket and leave on the day we first saw each other on the elevator, but strangely enough, he hadn't been able to. Someone or something was clearly intervening to make sure we'd get to know each other.

We talked for an entire second hour, and since I was hungry by then, I accepted his dinner invitation. Luckily, he didn't have a car, so I didn't have to worry about being chopped up and left in the trunk. In any case, he suggested a restaurant on the next block, within walking distance.

It was a strange evening. The more I liked what I was hearing, the more conflicted I felt in the face of my vow of chastity. When I got back to my room, I had a serious talk with God. I told him that I wasn't at all amused that he was putting me in this situation. If he was going to send me someone who would make the earth move, why did it have to be a gringo? "No," I told him. "Let's be honest. If it bothered you so much that I didn't go to mass, you

159

could have thought of some other prank to pull on me."

Bill and I had arranged to take a walk on the beach the next day. We went down the elevator, this time by agreement. The white sand was brilliant in the sun, the Caribbean was an intense blue, fish frolicked on the surface, and the birds sang sweetly. No, I told myself, this can't be love. It can't be.

To make a long story short, we spent two wonderful days on the island and said our goodbyes on Sunday with lumps in our throats, thinking that we'd never see each other again.

I arrived in San Antonio on Monday, and when I opened my email, I found not one or two but ten emails from him. He missed me, he said. I was beautiful, he added, and he'd never met anyone else like me, along with all sorts of other things that people say when they're in love.

Me in love? You must be kidding. These things only happen in movies. It's been nice, Mr. Architect, but that's as far as it goes. You in the north of the

United States and me in Colombia? Thanks for the flattery, but it's time to come back down to earth. I'm single because I've given up on men. I've had more than enough of their shenanigans, and I'm really not up for any more of that.

Two weeks after returning to Colombia I was back in the United States for Thanksgiving dinner with his family, and the rest is history.

https://www.youtube.com/watch?v=TpfWnH00ZO4

Coincidir (Silvio Rodríguez)

Epilogue

Two years before I met Bill, someone suggested I make a list of the qualities of my ideal man, and that's what I did. I wrote out a list on New Year's Eve, and just as the clock struck midnight, I slipped it into one of those books that you keep because you read it and liked it, but would probably never read again.

When I got home from Puerto Rico, though, I looked for the list and found it. Imagine my surprise when I discovered that with one exception, Bill had all the qualities I'd dreamed of.

Now I know that my list was useful only because of my own transformation, because I now understood that happiness comes not from outside but from within you, and that nobody can love you if you don't love yourself. Despite many hurdles and setbacks, I had learned to love myself and be my own best friend.

I learned that life is a reflection of what you see in it. If all you see is darkness, then all will in fact be dark. I recovered my lost optimism and laughed again. I'm not alone in the world anymore, but I don't really need anyone else to be myself. When I look in the mirror, I like what I see. And very softly, so He can barely hear me, I thank God for my time on earth.

Now I know and appreciate that even the darkest of nights is followed by a beautiful day. One must simply wait and hope. Someone cares about you and will give you all you need to grow.

https://www.youtube.com/watch?v=Vm5Dl1e10x4

Qué suerte he tenido de nacer (Alberto Cortez)

How lucky I have been to be born
By Alberto Cortés. Translated by Virginia Perez-
Santalla

How lucky I have been to be born!
Yes, how lucky I have been to be born
To shake the hand of a friend
And be able to attend as a witness
The miracle of each sunrise

How lucky I have been to be born
To have the option of the scale,
To weigh defeat and hope
With the glory and the fear of falling

How lucky I have been to be born
To understand that the honest and the wicked
Own the universe alike
Even though they differ in their beliefs

How lucky I have been to be born
To keep quiet when the most knowledgeable speaks
Learn to listen, that's the key
If knowledge is your intent

How lucky I have been to be born,
And I say it without false triumphalism
Total victory over my own self
Focuses in being and not being

How lucky I have been to be born
To sing to the people and to the rose
And the dog and love and anything
That my feelings may gather

164

How lucky I have been to be born
To have access to the fortune
Of being a river instead of being a lagoon
Of being rain instead of seeing it rain

How lucky I have been to be born
To eat the apple thoroughly
Without the ancient fear of the cassock
Or of Lucifer's final revenge

Yes, how lucky I have been to be born!
But I know, I well know...
That one day I will also die
And if now I live happy with my luck
God knows what I'll think when I am dying

Acknowledgements

This book wouldn't have seen the light of day if I hadn't been encouraged to write it by many people. It would be very hard to name them all, and it would be a serious oversight on my part to omit any of them. But you know who you are, and above all, you know that I'm deeply grateful to all of you.

To my family for sharing their lives with me. Without you my task would have been more difficult and perhaps less interesting.

To all the true friends I've found on this path.

To all my Maestros, those who've accompanied and taught me, even if they've occasionally had to knock some sense into my head.

To Lucho and Alba, a faithful presence in my life for 30 years.

To my dear friend the outstanding literary translator Vicky Roa, maria.v.roa@gmail.com, who

166

read the manuscript and patiently provided me with commentaries and suggestions.

To Andy Klatt, andy.klatt@gmail.com who did an admirable job translating it into English.

To my friend Virginia Perez-Santalla for her translation of *Qué suerte he tenido de nacer (How lucky I have been to be born)*, the poem that closes this book. How lucky I have been to have friends like her!

And finally, to my dogs. They have taught me to laugh at their antics and given me abundant love. I will always have a tail-wagging dog at my side.

The Spanish version of this book was completed in
May 2021.

olmuper@gmail.com

Made in the USA
Columbia, SC
16 August 2022